Praise for Weird and Wacky Holiday Marketing Guide Through the Years ...

"The COVID-19 pandemic has changed marketing forever. This 2021 13th ed. of Ginger Marks's classic series *Weird and Wacky Holiday Marketing Guide* takes users out of their comfort zone of traditional holiday marketing tools into the new normal world of virtual events which can be implemented across a host of social media platforms.

"It is well worth your time to navigate through all of the new opportunities for promotion in our continuing and post-pandemic reality."
—**Dr. Edward Wirth, Jr., President, EDW Consulting, Inc.**

"This book is a fun way to market just about anything. Organized by month, with month-long holidays, week-long holidays, and then daily holidays. Most of the holidays are so obscure that most people wouldn't be aware they even exist. But that is the point: taking a weird and wacky holiday and making a fun marketing post with it.

"Behind the monthly holidays is a section with sample posters and additional ideas that can be transferred to any other holiday, a sample press release, as well as links to companies and social media sites that might also help.

"I have gone through and highlighted holidays I want to promote for fun next time they roll around. The title is all about having a little fun while you market, and this book will not disappoint."
—**Pat Stanford, Author and Poet (2019 Edition)**

"This is such a wonderful resource. I love how Ginger has incorporated all different kinds of holidays to celebrate for many reasons. She also gives great input for Publishing! I am happy to have this resource!"
—**Lee Ann Mancini, Author of SeaKids Adventure Series (animated cartoon) (2019 Edition)**

Ginger Marks books are AMAZING! Her Marketing Guide is a MUST HAVE for those wanting to stand out in a crowd. All her books are wonderful. Ginger's Marketing Book is a PERFECT solution to all my sales and marketing needs. Don't miss out on her unique Marketing TIPS to think outside the box and stand out in a crowd. Thank you, Ginger Marks!
—**Jennifer P., Author/Illustrator (2019 Edition)**

"Ginger Marks' *Weird and Wacky Holiday Marketing Guide* is a compendium of ideas to market your product, tying it to state, national and international celebrations of every conceivable kind. The research done for this book is mind-boggling. The holidays are organized by month, and list month-long, week-long, and daily holidays. Appendix A provides a huge number of ready-made materials you can use for blog posts, flyers, press releases, etc. If you're looking to jump-start your marketing, you must get this book. Highly recommended."
—**A Writer (2018 Edition)**

"A Google Search on Steroids! Have you ever done a Google search while preparing a presentation and found an incredible list that helped you add lots of ideas to what you were doing? I have and know that having such a list always gives me lots of information to make my presentation more interesting and colorful.

"Ginger Marks' *2018 Weird and Wacky Holiday Marketing Guide* is just like having the results of a Google search, only it is like having such a list on steroids! The guide contains an overwhelming number of marketing ideas. The first 70 pages list national, international, and quite frankly, often quirky and humorous events which take place throughout the year, listed in month-to-month order. If humor is what you are looking for, you will learn that National Hermit Week falls in June, "Hot Enough for Ya Day" falls on July 23rd, and August 7th is known as the "Particularly Preposterous Packaging Day." These three dates are just samples of the hundreds (even maybe a thousand) of weird and wacky celebrations, festivals, and events that are included in Ginger Marks' 2018 guide.

"The second half of the book contains several appendices, which once again provides all kinds of marketing information. I can't imagine a business owner who couldn't find some great marketing ideas while looking through the first half of this book, or who couldn't find links to companies that might help his or her business in the second half of the book. There is so much information here. The *2018 Weird and Wacky Holiday Marketing Guide* is a terrific resource!"
—**Gary Ciesla (2018 Edition)**

As someone who's taught "Marketing Your Biz on a Shoestring" for years, I always note the value of fun/crazy/unusual holidays for adding to your marketing options. Ginger has put together a great guide that gives you EVERYTHING: serious holidays, regularly scheduled holidays, and just for fun stuff.
—**Wendy Meyeroff, WM Medical Communications, Inc. (2018 Edition)**

"Ginger Marks has put together a fantastic resource! If you are looking for outside of the box ideas for marketing as well as for celebrating, you are going to love the *Weird and Wacky Holiday Marketing Guide*. As a former elementary school teacher, I wish I had had a copy of this incredible resource when I was teaching. The month-long and week-long holidays, listed throughout this guide, could create the foundation for exciting study units."
—**D'vorah Lansky, M.Ed. Best-Selling author of Book Marketing Made Easy, www.BookMarketingMadeEasy.com (2016 Edition)**

"Great marketing tools for social media business exposure. Having multiple businesses and also doing websites, I found this book to be a wonderful asset for trying to come up with new "and different" ideas for marketing, especially on social media. Talk about having every holiday imaginable listed in this book!! There are also so many that it intrigues your interest to go off and further investigate on your own, after learning about them for the first time.

"I personally liked that at the end of the calendar month she adds some ideas on how to use these holidays to your advantage in marketing, but more importantly, she is always adding comments you can raise the money for charity or a good cause (not just to market your business but also help your community at the same time). If you have a business that is seeking attention on social media, I think this book will help you announce some totally Weird and Wacky facts for every day of the year, that will certainly get you noticed!! A wealth of resources here."
—**Cheryl (2018 Edition)**

"So much info in one book! As a business owner, it's difficult to stand out. With Ginger's guidance you can set yourself apart from the crowd. It's well-written and easy to follow. Tons and tons of info and well worth it!"
—**Patti Knoles, Virtual Graphic Arts Department (2017 Edition)**

"Awesome very practical and fun marketing ideas. Ginger Marks' *2018 Weird and Wacky Holiday Marketing Guide* is an amazing book and tool for me to use preparing speeches in my business. Using anecdotes from the book I can enhance my presentations to be much more fun and colorful and keep the audience entertained. I can't wait to show this book to my colleagues.

"There are numerous marketing ideas I never would have come up with on my own that I plan to use in my business social media which should really help engagement. I love that I can get new ideas all year long!"

—Rachel I (2018 Edition)

2021 Weird & Wacky HOLIDAY MARKETING GUIDE
13th Edition
Your business marketing calendar of ideas

Ginger Marks

DocUmeant *Publishing*
244 5th Avenue
Suite G-200
NY, NY 10001
646-233-4366
www.DocUmeantPublishing.com

2021 Weird and Wacky Holiday Marketing Guide, Volume 13
Published by
DocUmeant Publishing
244 5th Ave, Ste G–200
NY, NY 10001

646-233-4366

Weird & Wacky Holiday Marketing Guide, Volume 13

Published by DocUmeant Publishing
244 5th Ave, Ste G–200
NY, NY 10001
646-233-4366

© Copyright 2021 Ginger Marks. All rights reserved.

No portion of this book may be duplicated in any way by any means, electronically or manually without the expressed written permission of the author, except for personal use. Address all comments and questions to Ginger.Marks@DocUmeantDesigns.com.

Editor Wendy VanHatten
VanHatten Writing Services
wvanhatten@gmail.com

Layout and Design Ginger Marks
DocUmeant Designs
www.DocUmeantDesigns.com

Library of Congress: 2020951958

ISBN: 978-1-950075-33-1

Digital: 978-1-950075-34-8

Contents

Introduction vii

Annual Dates of Note 1
    United Nations International Year of Fruits and Vegetables 1
    International Year for the Elimination of Child Labor 1
    International Year of Creative Economy for Sustainable Development 1
    International Year of Peace and Trust 2
    Chinese Year of the Ox 2
        Lucky Signs 2
        Lucky Directions 2
        Strengths 2
        Weaknesses 2
        Best Jobs and Careers 2
        Matches 2
        Avoid: Tiger, Dragon, Horse, Sheep 3
        Rat's Personality by Blood Type 3
        Avoid: Tiger, Dragon, Horse, Sheep 3
        Rat's Personality by Blood Type 3

JANUARY 5
    Month-Long Holidays 5
    Week-Long Holidays 5
    Daily Holidays 5
    Holiday Marketing Ideas 7

FEBRUARY 9
    Month-Long Holidays 9
    Week-Long Holidays 9
    Daily Holidays 9
    Holiday Marketing Ideas 11

MARCH 13
    Month-Long Holidays 13
    Week-Long Holidays 13
    Daily Holidays 14
    Holiday Marketing Ideas 16

APRIL 19
    Month-Long Holidays 19
    Week-Long Holidays 19
    Daily Holidays 20
    Holiday Marketing Ideas 22

MAY — 24
- Month-Long Holidays — 24
- Week-Long Holidays — 24
- Daily Holidays — 25
- Holiday Marketing Ideas — 27

JUNE — 29
- Month-Long Holidays — 29
- Week-Long Holidays — 29
- Daily Holidays — 29
- Holiday Marketing Ideas — 31

JULY — 34
- Month-Long Holidays — 34
- Week-Long Holidays — 34
- Daily Holidays — 34
- Holiday Marketing Ideas — 36

AUGUST — 38
- Month-Long Holidays — 38
- Week-Long Holidays — 38
- Daily Holidays — 38
- Holiday Marketing Ideas — 40

SEPTEMBER — 43
- Month-Long Holidays — 43
- Week-Long Holidays — 43
- Daily Holidays — 44
- Holiday Marketing Ideas — 45

OCTOBER — 48
- Month-Long Holidays — 48
- Week-Long Holidays — 48
- Daily Holidays — 49
- Holiday Marketing Ideas — 51

NOVEMBER — 53
- Month-Long Holidays — 53
- Week-Long Holidays — 53
- Daily Holidays — 53
- Holiday Marketing Ideas — 55

DECEMBER — 57
- Month-Long Holidays — 57
- Week-Long Holidays — 57
- Daily Holidays — 57
- Holiday Marketing Ideas — 59

Appendix A: SAMPLES ---------------------------------- 61
   Sample Press Release 61
   Random Act of Kindness Card 62
   National JoyGerm Day Graphics 63
   Extraterrestrial Culture Day Social Media Graphic 65
   Simplify Your Life Tips 66
   Balloon Piggy Bank 67
   20 Famous Pigs 69
   National Pig Day Graphics 70
   Dress in Blue Graphic 72
   Pecan Recipes 73
   The Grass is Always Browner on the Other Side of the Fence Day Social Media Graphic. 77
   Blah! Blah! Blah! Day Social Media Graphic 78
   Public Schools Day Social Media Graphic 79
   Hat Etiquette 80
   National Odometer Day Event Flyer 81
   International Learn to Swim Day Social Media Graphic 82
   "Tear Down This Wall" Day Social Media Graphic 83
   National Prune Day Health Benefits 84
   National Prune Day Social Media Graphic 85
   National Lighthouse Day Social Media Graphic 87
   10 Health Benefits of Chocolate 88
   National Dog Day Social Media Graphic 89
   Organize a Food Drive 91
      Tip Sheet: Meeting an Organization's Needs 94
      Tips on Managing Volunteers 95
      Tips on Generating Publicity 95
      Sample Food Drive Food List 97
      Food Drive Flyer 98
      SNAP Flyer 99
   World Smile Day Social Media Graphic 100
   World Purse Day Social Media Image 101
   Saxophone Day Graphic 102
   National Lard Day Social Media Graphics 103
   National Candy Cane Day Card 105
   National Candy Cane Day Facts 106
   Candy Cane Recipes 107

Appendix B: Social Media Image Size Guide ----------------- 113
   FACEBOOK 113
   LINKEDIN 113
   YOUTUBE 114
   INSTAGRAM 114
   TWITTER 114
   PINTEREST 114
   TUMBLER 115

GOOGLE+ 115
ELLO 115
SNAPCHAT 115
    Chinese Social Media 116
WECHAT 116
WEIBO 116

Appendix C: LINKS — 117
Link Checker 117
Article Marketing Sites 117
Auto Responder Services 117
Books and Movies 118
Greeting Card Companies 118
Podcast Directories 118
Promotional Product Supply Companies 119
Quote Sources 119
Stock Photos 120
Teleconference Companies 121
Virtual Assistant Companies 121
Webinar Services 121

Appendix D: RESOURCES — 123
Food Drive Resources 123

About the Author — 125

Additional Works — 127

Weird and Wacky Holiday Marketing Guide Archive — 135

Introduction

Events are one of the smartest prescriptions for slumping sales and for maintaining a healthy business. It's not enough anymore to merely have goods on the shelf and open the doors on time every day. We all need to reinvent our businesses to keep them thriving and healthy. And, that is just what this book helps you achieve.

This unique marketing book continues to win awards year after year and remains a #1 Best-Seller in the Business Marketing genre. Highly praised by marketing experts and now entering its second decade, this book offers more fun and easy marketing ideas exclusively penned for the calendar year 2021. Now you can grow your business with strategies built around wacky holidays, observed throughout the world, for the entire 2021 calendar year. If you missed the premier 2009 issue or want to complete your collection, all previous and unique yearly editions are available at http://www.HolidayMarketingGuide.com.

As *Weird and Wacky Holiday Marketing Guide* is read and used internationally, I have included many International holidays.

To take advantage of the information provided, pick a day and discover the unusual holidays celebrated on that date. Then, read the corresponding month's "Holiday Marketing Ideas" section to find a simple implementation or allow it to open your creative mind and think of some of your own.

Please note that the asterisk (*) in front of a holiday means a specific holiday is celebrated on that numerical date each year. For example, Christmas Day is December 25 no matter what day that falls on during the calendar week.

Here's another exceptional marketing idea for you I discovered when visiting BrownieLocks.com back in 2009, and which is now listed in the official *Chase Calendar of Events* which I cull from every year. Bonza Bottler Days™—the day is the same as the month it is in. That equates to: 1/1, 2/2, 3/3, etc. There is one in every month. There you have it; another extra fine excuse for an event to boost your notoriety and sales each and every month!

This is by no means a comprehensive edition. I have made all attempts to ensure the accuracy of the contents. If you encounter errors or know of a holiday that needs to be included, please let me know so they can be addressed in future editions. But remember, if your suggested holiday addition is not listed in the official *Chase Calendar of Events* it is not eligible for inclusion.

Read on, have fun, initiate your own version of these holidays, and reap the benefit for your business.

Ginger Marks

P.S. The *Weird and Wacky Holiday Marketing Companion Playbook*. This tool is intended to help you to create, organize, and put the FUN back into your marketing plan. Each monthly calendar offers space for you to begin your planning and keep all your notes in one handy book. Since each year the physical calendar days rotate, I have left the date numbers blank to enable you to make use of this *Companion Playbook* beginning today.

Annual Dates of Note

United Nations International Year of Fruits and Vegetables

The International Year of Fruits and Vegetables invites the international community to raise public awareness and direct policy attention to the nutritional and health benefits of fruits and vegetables and to the reduction of their loss and waste. Recognizing the contribution of fruits and vegetables to the food security, generation of income and employment of small holders and family farmers, the year emphasizes the empowerment of women through education, recognizing their role in sustainable farming practices, and is conceived to have a positive impact in reducing hunger and poverty, enhancing food and nutrition security, improving livelihoods, and contributing to better natural resource management. For information on all of the International Year designations visit www.un.org.

International Year for the Elimination of Child Labor

The International Year for the Elimination of Child Labor promotes activities aimed at raising awareness of the importance of the eradication of child labor and sharing best practices in this regard. Children aged five to 17 are considered child laborers when they are too young to work or are involved in hazardous activities that compromise their physical, mental, social, or educational development. The International Labor Organization's *World Report on Child Labour* of 2013 documents 265 million children, or 17 percent of the worldwide child population, as child laborers. Data collected by UNICEF from 2010 to 2018 finds that one in four children in the world's poorest countries is engaged in child labor; it is most prevalent in sub-Saharan Africa, where 29 percent of children work.

International Year of Creative Economy for Sustainable Development

This year is dedicated to fostering economic growth and innovation, eradicating poverty, creating productive employment for all, and improving the quality of life and empowerment of women and your people.

International Year of Peace and Trust

This year aims to mobilize international efforts through the year to promote peace and trust among nations on the basis of political dialogue, mutual understanding, and cooperation in order to build sustainable global peace, solidarity and harmony.

Chinese Year of the Ox[1]

This is the Year of Metal Ox, starting from Feb. 12, 2021 (Chinese New Year) and lasting to Jan. 31, 2022.

Ox is the second in the 12-year cycle of Chinese zodiac sign. Years of the Ox include 1913, 1925, 1937, 1949, 1961, 1973, 1985, 1997, 2009, 2021, 2033 …

Oxen used to be capable farming tools in agricultural society, which attach to the symbol of diligence, persistence, and honesty. People born in the Year of Ox are probably tardy in action, but industrious and cautious. Most of them are conservative and hold their faith firmly.

Lucky Signs
Lucky Numbers: 1, 9

Lucky Colors: red, blue, purple

Lucky Flowers: tulip, evergreen, peach blossom

Lucky Directions
Southeast, south, and north

Strengths
Honest, industrious, patient, cautious, level-headed, strong-willed, persistent

Weaknesses
Obstinate, inarticulate, prudish, distant

Best Jobs and Careers
Best Jobs: Lawyer, doctor, teacher, technician, politician, office clerk, consultant …

Best Working Partners: Rat, Rooster, Snake

Best Age to Start a Business: 30 – 40

Best Career Fields: Building Material Field

Matches
Perfect: Rat, Snake, Rooster

---

1   Travel China Guide. https://www.travelchinaguide.com/intro/social_customs/zodiac/ox.htm

They are quite compatible, deeply attracted by each other. They are both responsible, willing to share the family duty. Besides, loyalty and faith are the key factors to their happy marriage.

Avoid: Tiger, Dragon, Horse, Sheep

They will stick on their own opinions and ideas, and they both can hardly give in. They aren't used to forgiveness, and squabbles lead to their relationship reaction.

Rat's Personality by Blood Type

Blood Type O: They are bright and frank, which makes them to be reliable partners. Uprightness and kindness make them popular.

Blood Type A: They are cautious and careful in work, and they can be good advisors.

Blood Type B: They are highly esteemed, and they are always the one that come up with novelty ideas in a group.

Blood Type AB: They are strong-minded and will not easily be defeated by any difficulties.

Avoid: Tiger, Dragon, Horse, Sheep

They will stick on their own opinions and ideas, and they both can hardly give in. They aren't used to forgiveness, and squabbles lead to their relationship reaction.

Rat's Personality by Blood Type

Blood Type O: They are bright and frank, which makes them to be reliable partners. Uprightness and kindness make them popular.

Blood Type A: They are cautious and careful in work, and they can be good advisors.

Blood Type B: They are highly esteemed, and they are always the one that come up with novelty ideas in a group.

Blood Type AB: They are strong-minded and will not easily be defeated by any difficulties.

JANUARY

Jan 6 – Feb 16 Carnival Season
Jan 7 – Feb 16 Germany: Munich Fasching Carnival
Jan 20 – Feb 19 Aquarius the Water Carrier
Jan 31 – Feb 17 Canada: Winterlude

Month-Long Holidays

Be Kind to Food Servers Month, Book Blitz Month, International Child-Centered Divorce Month, International Creativity Month, National Cheesy Sock Month, National Clean Up Your Computer Month, National Conscience Month, National Glaucoma Awareness Month, National Hot Tea Month, National Mentoring Month, National Radon Action Month, National Skating Month, National Slavery and Human Trafficking Prevention Month, National Volunteer Blood Donor Month, Oatmeal Month, Worldwide Rising Star Month

Week-Long Holidays

Jan 1 – 2 Taiwan: Foundation Days
Jan 2 – 8 Someday We'll Laugh About This Week
Jan 11 – 17 Cuckoo Dancing Week
Jan 16 – 17 Bald Eagle Appreciation Days
Jan 17 – 23 Hunt for Happiness Week
Jan 18 – 25 Week of Christian Unity
Jan 24 – 30 Clean Out Your Inbox Week, Idiom Week, Snowcare for Troops Awareness Week
Jan 28 – Feb 7 Sundance Film Festival (subject to change)

Daily Holidays

1. *Bonza Bottler Day™, Canada: Polar Bear Swim 2021, *Copyright Revision Law Signed (1976), Cuba: Liberation Day, Czech-Slovak Divorce (1993), *Ellis Island Opened (1892), *Emancipation Proclamation Takes Effect (1863), *Euro Introduced (1999), *First Baby Boomer Born (1946), *Frankenstein (1818), *Haiti: Independence Day, *National Environmental Policy Act (1970), *New Year's Day, *Paul Revere Birthday (1735), *Betsy Ross (1752), Russia New Year's Day Observance, Saint Basil's Day, Sudan: Independence Day, *Z Day
2. 55-MPH Speed Limit (1974), Isaac Asimov Birth (1920), Earth at Perihelion, Haiti: Ancestor's Day, *Happy Mew Year for Cats Day, Japan: Kakizome, Switzerland: Berchtoldstag
3. Memento Mori, JRR Tolkien Birth (1892), Saint Geneviève Feast Day
4. *Amnesty for Polygamists (1893), *Louise Braille Birth (1809), *Dimpled Chad Day, *Myanmar: Independence Day, *Isaac Newton Birth (1643), *Pop Music Chart Introduced (1936), *Trivia Day, *World Braille Day, World's Tallest Building Dedicated (2010)

5. *Alvin Ailey Birth (1931), *Five-Dollar-a-Day Minimum Wage Day (1914), National Bird Day, Twelfth Night
6. *Armenian Christmas, *Epiphany or Twelfth Day, New Mexico Admission Day, *Three Kings Day
7. *First Balloon Fight Across the English Channel (1785), *International Programmers' Day, Japan: Nanakusa, *National Bobblehead Day, Orthodox Christmas, Russia: Christmas Observed, Transatlantic Phoning (1927)
8. Argyle Day, Greece: Midwife's Day or Women's Day, *National JoyGerm Day, *Show-and-Tell at Work Day, *War on Poverty (1964)
9. *Aviation in America (1793), *Panama: Martyrs' Day
10. League of Nations Founding (1920), Switzerland: Meitlisunntic, Women's Suffrage Amendment Introduced in Congress (1878)
11. England: Plough Monday, Japan: Coming-of-Age Day, Morocco: Independence Day, National Clean-Off-Your-Desk Day, Nepal: National Unity Day, U.S. Surgeon Declares Cigarettes Hazardous (1964)
12. *Haiti Earthquake Day (2010), National Hot Tea Day, Poetry at Work Day, Tanzania: Zanzibar Revolution Day
13. Norway: Tyvendedagen, *Radio Broadcasting Day (1910), Russian Old New Year's Eve, Sweden: St. Knut's Day, Togo: Liberation Day
14. *Arnold Benedict Day, *Ratification Day, Uzbekistan: Army Day, World Logic Day
15. *Alpha Kappa Alpha Sorority Day, Arbor Day in Florida, International Fetish Day, National Bagel Day, Quarterly Estimated Federal Income Tax Day (also Apr 15, Jun 15, and Sep 15)
16. *Appreciate a Dragon Day, *Civil Service Day, El Salvador: National Day of Peace, Japan Haru-No-Yabuiri, Malawi: John Chilembwe Day, National Nothing Day, National Quinoa Day, *Religious Freedom Day
17. Anne Brontë Day, The Business of America Quote Day (1925), *Cable Car Day (1871), *Al Capone Day, *Ben Franklin Day (1706), International Mentoring Day, Japan: Earthquake Day, *Judgment Day, Kid Inventors' Day, Mexico: Blessing of the Animals at the Cathedral, Poland: Liberation Day, Popeye Day, Saint Anthony's Day, Southern California Earthquake Day (1994)
18. Martin Luther King, Jr. Birth Observed (1986), Lewis and Clark Day, *Pooh Day
19. Ethiopia: Timket, Robert E. Lee Day, National Popcorn Day, Edgar Allen Poe Day
20. Azerbaijan: Martyrs' Day, Brazil: San Sebastian's Day, Guinea-Bissau: National Heroes Day, Inauguration Day, Lesotho: Army Day, US Hostages in Iran Released (1981), US Revolutionary War Ends Day (1783)
21. Fist Supersonic Concorde Flight (1976), Get to Know Your Customers Day (third Thursday of each quarter is set aside to get to know your customers even better), Kiwanis International Founding (1915), National Hug Your Puppy Day, *National Hugging Day
22. *Answer Your Cat's Question Day, Laugh-In Day, *Roe vs. Wade Decision (1973), *Saint Vincent: Feast Day, Ukraine: Ukrainian Day
23. Bulgaria: Babin Den (Midwives/Grandmother's Day), Eagle Day, Local Quilt Shop Day, *National Handwriting Day, National Pie Day, Snowplow Mailbox Hockey Day
24. *Belly Laugh Day, California Gold Discovery Day, *Beer Can Day (1935), *National Compliment Day, United Nations: International Day of Education, World Day for African and Afrodescendant Culture
25. *Around the World in 72 Days (1890), Bubble Wrap® Appreciation Day, *Macintosh Debuts (1984), *A Room of One's Own Day, Saint Dwynwen's Day

26. Australia: Australia Day, Dental Drill Day, Dominican Republic: National Holiday, India: Republic Day, Indian Earthquake (2001), Rocky Mountain National Park Day
27. Canadian Caper/Operation Argo (40th Anniversary, 1980), Germany: Day of Remembrance for Victims of Nazism, Leningrad Liberated (1944), *Mozart Day, National Geographic Society Founded (1888) *Thomas Crapper Day, United Kingdom: Holocaust Memorial Day, United Nations: International Day of Commemoration in Memory of the Victims of the Holocaust, *Vietnam Peace Day
28. *Challenger Space Shuttle Explosion (1986), Data Privacy Day, Israeli Siege of Suez City Ends (1974), Tu B'Shvat
29. *Curmdgeons Day, W.C. Fields Day, National Preschool Fitness Day, *Seeing Eye Dog Day
30. Ireland: Bloody Sunday, Inane Answering Message Day, National Croissant Day, National Seed Swap Day, World Leprosy Day
31. Carol Channing Day (1921), *First Social Security Check Issued (1940), The Grammy Awards, *Inspire Your Heart with the Arts Day, Nauru: National Holiday, 2021 Pro Bowl

Holiday Marketing Ideas

Be Kind to Food Servers Month — These hard-working service professionals are weathering the COVID-19 storm and deserve our appreciation. So, to show your appreciation for their diligence, take every opportunity you can to thank them for their service. One suggestion I offer is to hand them a branded 'RAK' (random act of kindness) card. You'll find one I created which you can customize with your logo in the Samples Appendix. In the 2014 edition of this book series you will find a list of ideas that you can do as RAKs which will give you opportunities to share your RAK cards.

Jan 5 National Bird Day — Do I hear a Twitter in the house? Get your hashtags out and fly them around the web as you celebrate this Weird & Wacky holiday. If you are a teacher or because of COVID-19 you are still homeschooling, you might want to get the true story of Lucky, a parrot who is captured in the wild and eventually gains her freedom. To learn more about this avian star get your copy of Lucky the Lorikeet's which can be found on Amazon. The link to their website is in the Resources Appendix.

Jan 8 National JoyGerm Day — This is a germ you are sure to want to catch! Unlike COVID-19 the JoyGerm is a wonderful infection that you should infect all those around you with as soon and as often as possible. Spread some cheer in big and little ways throughout the day. A branded graphic or two is a good start. Posting branded positive quotes are also an option to easily celebrate today. But be sure you spend the day treating others whose lives you will touch with respect and kindness. That will all go a long way to infecting those who you'll meet. I encourage you to spread the JoyGerm today! I have created some images you can use that you'll find in the Samples Appendix and links to quote websites in the Links Appendix.

Jan 14 World Logic Day — World Logic Day has been on the calendar since 2019. Humanity, and thus human logic, is associated with concepts such as consciousness, knowledge, and reason. As you consider how to promote your business while celebrating this prestigious holiday take the time to ponder whether starting a mentorship or think tank group would be a good fit for you. You could have a contest and offer to mentor the winner. That's sure to garner some intelligent business minded individuals to pay attention.

Some business owners who are life, career, or spiritual coaches would do well to consider this a marketing goldmine. Host a webinar or post branded tips on social media to share your concepts with your audience. These are not hard to accomplish. However, be sure to start planning early so that you have time to put together your promotional graphics and develop a team to help you get the word out.

Jan 24 Belly Laugh Day—No kidding! This definitely classifies as a Weird & Wacky holiday. On this day of mirth share your favorite jokes, post a humorous image, or better yet, have others post their own Weird & Wacky selves from a previous era. You could turn this into a contest if you are up to the challenge. But be sure your prizes are of the sort that would cause a guffaw or two.

It is said that laughter is good for the soul. Having a good chuckle causes the tissue lining our blood vessels to expand increase blood flow. This makes us feel more positive, boosts our immune systems, increases pain tolerance, and generally just makes us feel happier and more energetic! So, join in the frivolity and offer up a chuckle or two. At the very least, wish everyone a happy Belly Laugh Day.

FEBRUARY

Feb 17 – Apr 3 Lent
Feb 11 – 21 Germany: Berlin International Film Festival

Month-Long Holidays

African American Cultural Heritage Month, AMD/Low Vision Awareness Month, *American Heart Month, Bake for Family Fun Month, Feline Fix By Five Month, International Boost Self-Esteem Month, Library Lovers' Month, Marfan Syndrome Awareness Month, *National African American History Month, National Bird-Feeding Month, National Black History Month, National Cherry Month, National Condom Month, National Goat Yoga Month, National Mend a Broken Heart Month, National Parent Leadership Month®, National Pet Dental Health Month, National Time Management Month, Plant the Seeds of Greatness Month, Return Shopping Carts to the Supermarket Month, Spay/Neuter Awareness Month, Spunky Old Broads Month, Wise Health Care Consumer Month

Week-Long Holidays

Feb 1 – 7 African Heritage and Health Week
Feb 8 – 13 Freelance Writers Appreciation Week
Feb 8 – 14 Love a Mensch Week Love May Make the World Go 'Round, But Laughter Keeps us from Getting Dizzy Week
Feb 9 – 11 World AG Expo
Feb 12 – 14 Gold Rush Days
Feb 12 – 15 Great Backyard Bird Count
Feb 14 – 20 International Flirting Week
Feb 14 – 16 Shrovetide
Feb 15 – 16 Germany and Austria: Fasching
Feb 21 – 27 Build a Better Trade Show Image Week, National Engineers Week

Daily Holidays

1. Car Insurance Day, *Robinson Crusoe Day, Freedom Day, G.I. Joe Day, Greensboro Sit-In (60th Anniversary, 1960), *Betsy Ross Birthday (1752), Space Shuttle *Columbia* Disaster (2003), St. Laurent, Louis Stephen Day
2. *Bonza Bottler Day™, *Candlemas Day or Presentation of the Lord, *Groundhog Day, Hedgehog Day, *Imbolc, Luxembourg: Candlemas, Mexico: Dia de la Candelaria, *The Record of a Sneeze" (1893), Sled Dogs Save Nome (1925)
3. *"The Day the Music Died" (1959), *Four Chaplains Memorial Day, *Income Tax Birthday, Mozambiue: Heroes' Day, National Girls and Women in Sports Day, National Signing Day, Vietnam: National Holiday

4. Angola: Armed Struggle Day, Apache Wars Begin (1868), *Facebook Launches (2004), Medjool Date Day, *Rosa Parks Birthday (1913), Sri Lanka: Independence Day, *USO Founded (1941), World Cancer Day
5. Bubble Gum Day, Canada: Winterlude, *Family Leave Bill Signing (1993), Longest War in History Ends (31985), Mexico: Constitution Day, National Wear Red Day, *Weatherperson's Day
6. New Zealand: Waitangi Day, "Babe" Ruth Birthday (1895), Take Your Child to the Library Day, United Nations: International Day of Zero Tolerance for Female Genital Mutilation
7. *Ballet Day, *Chaplin's "Tramp" Day (1914), *Charles Dickens (1812), Grenada: Independence Day, Man Day, National Black HIV/AIDS Awareness Day, Switzerland: Homstom, *Wave Your Fingers at Your Neighbor Day
8. *Boy Scouts of America Day (1910), Japan: Hari-Kuyo (Festival of Broken Needles), Slovenia: Culture Day
9. *Beatles Day (1964), Extraterrestrial Culture Day, *Gypsy Rose Lee (1914), Lebanon: Saint Maron's Day, National Pizza Day, Read in the Bathtub Day, *Ernest Tubb (1914)
10. *"All the News That's Fit to Print" Slogan (1897), *First Computer Chess Victory over Human (1996), *First WWII Medal of Honor (1942), *Charles Lamb (1775), *Plimsoll Day, Treaty of Paris (1763), United Nations: World Pulses Day
11. Cameroon: Youth Day, *Thomas Edison Birthday (1847), *First Woman Episcopal Bishop (1989), Get Out Your Guitar Day, Iran: Victory of Islamic Revolution, *Japan: National Foundation Day, *National Shut-In Visitation Day, *Pro Sports Wives Day, *Satisfied Staying Single Day, United Nations: International Day of Women and Girls in Science, Vatican City: Independence Day, White Shirt Day
12. * Chinese New Year, *Dracula Day, *International Darwin Day, Abraham Lincoln (1809) and Birthplace Cabin Wreath Laying Day, Myanmar: Union Day, NAACP Founded (1909), *Oglethorpe Day, *Safetpup® Birthday, Utah: Women Given the Vote (1870)
13. Dresden Firebombing (1945), *First Magazine Published in America (1741), *Get a Different Name Day, World Radio Day
14. Arizona: Admission Day, Daytona 500, *ENAIC Computer Introduced (1946), Fasching Sunday, *Ferris Wheel Day, *First African American To Be Recorded on Vinyl (1920), *First Presidential Photograph (1849), *League of Women Voters Formed (1920), National Donor Day, Race Relations Day, *Saint Valentine`s Day, Space Milestone: 100th Space Walk (2001)
15. *Susan B Anthony Birthday (1820), World *Asteroid Near Miss Day, *Canada: Maple Leaf Flag Adopted (1910), *Chelyabinsky Meteor Explosion (2013), *Galileo Galilei Birthday (1564), Iceland: Bun Day, Love Reset Day, *Lupercalia, Presidents`Day, Remember the *Maine* Day (1898), *Serbia: National Day, Shrove Monday, George Washington`s Birthday Observed
16. Iceland: Bursting Day, Lithuania: Independence Day, Mardi Gras, Paczki Day, Shorve Tuesday
17. Ash Wednesday, *League of United Latin American Citizens (LULAC) Founded (1927), *My Way Day, *National PTA Founders' Day (1897)
18. Gambia: Independence Day, Nepal: National Democracy Day, George Peabody (1795), *Pluto Discovery Day (1930)
19. *Japanese Internment (1942), *Knights of Pythias Founding (1864), Skate Shop Day, *US Landing on Iwo Jima (1945)
20. Ansel Adams Day (1902), Closest Approach of a Comet to Earth (1491), *Northern Hemisphere Hoodie-Hoo Day, *United Nations: World Day for Social Justice, World Pangolin Day
21. Bangladesh: Martyrs Day, *United Nations: International Mother Language Day, *Washington Monument Dedicated (1885)

22. Florida Acquired by US (1819), Montgomery Boycott Arrests (1956), National Margarita Day, Saint Lucia: Independence Day, *George Washington`s Birthday (1732)
23. Brunei Darussalam: National Day, *Curling is Cool Day, Diesel Engine Day, Guyana: Anniversary of Republic, George Handel Day (1685) *Iwo Jima Day (1945), Japan: Birthday of the Emperor, Russia: Defender of the Fatherland Day, Single-Tasking Day, World Spay Day
24. Estonia: Independence Day, Georgian Calendar Day, Mexico: Flag Day
25. Clay Becomes Heavyweight Champ (1964), Digital Learning Day, Introduce a Girl to Engineering Day (Discovere Girl Day), Kuwait: National Day, National Chili Day, Ta'anit Esther
26. China, Taiwan, Korea: Lantern Festival, *FCC (Federal Communications Commission) created (1934), *For Pete's Sake Day, Grand Canyon National Park Established (1919), Kuwait: Liberation Day, Purim, *Levi Strauss Day, World Trade Center Bombing of 1993
27. Dominican Republic: Independence Day, International Polar Bear Day, Henry Wadsworth Longfellow (1807), Open that Bottle Night, World Sword Swallowers Day
28. Floral Design Day, *National Tooth Fairy Day, Taiwan: 288 Memorial Day

Holiday Marketing Ideas

National Goat Yoga Month — This month celebrate this absolutely Weird & Wacky holiday with sharing photos of yourself in various yoga poses, with, or around, a goat (even a stuffed one will do). The mirth continues when you have a photo op contest. The most unusual, or the cutest, or any number of reasons the photo can be chosen as the winner can make your photo event both hilarious and fun. If you don't believe me, check out Goat Yoga's website at https://goatyoga.com/ where you will find a gallery and information about this zany holiday.

Feb 1 G.I. Joe Day — This holiday is intended to celebrate the Hasbro toy, but why not take it a step further and celebrate our hardworking, loyal real G.I. Joes (and Janes). Thank them for their service with social media graphics that you have branded to your business or tweet your gratitude. Better even still, gather a few like-minded business owners and send care packages to a company or troupe stationed overseas. If you want to keep it local, volunteering at your local veteran's hospital or organization would be a wonderful alternative.

Feb 9 Extraterrestrial Culture Day — Expecting ET to drop in for tea might not be the thing to do today, but Extraterrestrial Culture Day exists *"to celebrate and honor all past, present and future extraterrestrial visitors in ways to enhance relationships among all citizens of the cosmos, known and unknown."* The day could be spent reading a book about aliens or the Roswell incident which was the reason this holiday was named. Consider binge watching television shows such as *Roswell* or *Roswell, New Mexico*, or a documentary series like *Ancient Aliens*. There also is long list of alien movies. Some classics include *Alien*, *E.T.*, *War of the Worlds*, and *Close Encounters of the Third Kind*. Then there's always *Star Wars* and *Star Trek*. This can be done with a group of friends or colleagues. Don't forget to post on social media your branded holiday graphic. Check the Samples Appendix for one you can brand and use to your delight.

Feb 14 National Donor Day — If you are up to the task why not volunteer to help people understand the importance of signing their organ donor agreement. You don't have to wait for your death either, you can actually be a 'living donor' and share a kidney or other tissue that could save someone's life. Gather a group of like-minded business owners and work with a hospital or clinic to get this done. Be sure to let the media know what you and your group are up to. They love feel-good stories about locals, and you could end up getting great press for you and your friends' businesses! If you are a tweeter be sure to use the hashtag #StartTheConversation.

Feb 27 International Polar Bear Day — Today we celebrate the polar bear and their dwindling numbers due to loss of habitat. However, it's not just polar bears that are suffering. We should all pay attention to the threats of climate change that everyone faces. So, gather some facts and put together some tips and graphics that you can share on your social media channels.

Alternatively, you might consider traits about the polar bear. Host an event that focuses on staying in shape, or eating properly, maybe even coming out of hibernation to seek success. Give it some thought, and you might just come up with a few terrific event ideas.

MARCH

Mar 6 – 21 Iditarod Trail Sled Dog Race
Mar 13 – Apr 15 Deaf History Month
Mar 15 – Apr 23 Orthodox Lent
Mar 21 – Apr 3 Passiontide
Mar 29 – Apr 4 Consider Christianity Week
Mar 30 – Apr 2 Italy: Bologna Children's Book Fair
Mar 30 – Apr 5 Mule Day

Month-Long Holidays

Alport Syndrome Awareness Month, *American Red Cross Month, Clap 4 Health Month, Colorectal Cancer Education and Awareness Month, Credit Education Month, Employee Spirit Month, Humorists Are Artists Month (HAAM), International Ideas Month, International Mirth Month, *Irish American Heritage Month, March Frozen Food Month, Music In Our Schools Month, National Clean Up Your IRS Act Month, National Colorectal Cancer Awareness Month, National Kidney Month, National Multiple Sclerosis Education and Awareness Month, National Nutrition Month®, National Peanut Month, National Umbrella Month, National Women's History Month, Optimism Month, Paws to Read Month, Play-the-Recorder Month, Poison Prevention Awareness Month, Red Cross Month, Save the Vaquita Month, Social Work Month, *Women's History Month, Workplace Eye Wellness Month, Worldwide Home Schooling Awareness Month, Youth Art Month

Week-Long Holidays

Mar 1 – 5 National School Breakfast Week
Mar 1 – 7 National Cheerleading Week, Return the Borrowed Books Week, Will Eisner Week
Mar 3 – 6 Association of Writers and Writing Programs Conference and Bookfair
Mar 4 – 7 Emerald City Comic Con
Mar 5 – 6 National Day of Unplugging
Mar 5 – 7 Aldo Leopold Weekend, International Festival of Owls
Mar 5 – 14 England: Words by the Water: A Festival of Words and Ideas
Mar 7 – 13 Celebrate You Name Week, Termite Awareness Week, Words Matter Week
Mar 9 – 11 London Book Fair
Mar 15 – 21 Brain Awareness Week, International Teach Music Week, United Kingdom: Shakespeare Week
Mar 11 – 17 Turkey Vultures Return to the Living Sign
Mar 20 – 21 Military Through the Ages
Mar 21 – 27 Consider Christianity Week, National Animal Poison Prevention Week, National Poison Prevention Week, National Protocol Officers Week, Passion Week, United Nations: Week

of Solidarity with the Peoples Struggling Against Racism and Racial Discrimination, World Folk Tales and Fables Week
Mar 26 – 28 Chicago Comic and Entertainment Expo (C2E2)
Mar 28 – Apr 3 Holy Week
Mar 28 – Apr 4 Pesach or Passover

Daily Holidays

1. Australia: Eight Hour Day or Labor Day, Baby Sleep Day, Bosnia and Herzegovina: Independence Day, Ralph Waldo Emerson Birthday (1914), Guam: Discovery Day or Magellan Day, *Iceland: Beer Day, Japan: Omizutori (Water-Drawing Festival), Korea: Samiljol or Independence Movement Day, Land Mine Ban Day, National Horse Protection Day (World Horse Day), National Pig Day, Paraguay: National Heroes' Day, Peace Corps Day, Plan a Solo Vacation Day, Refired, Not Retired, Day, Switzerland: Chalandra Marz, Wales: Saint David's Day, World Compliment Day, Zero Discrimination Day
2. Ethiopia: Adwa Day, *Highway Numbers Day (1925), *King Kong Day, NEA's Read Across America Day, Peace Corps Day, Texas Independence Day, Town Meeting Day
3. Alexander Graham Bell Birthday (1847), *Bonza Bottler Day™, Bulgaria: Liberation Day, Hin-Mah-Too-Yah-Lat-Kekt Birthday (1840), International Ear Care Day, Japan: Hina Matsuri (Doll Festival), Malawi: Martyr's Day, National Anthem Day, Simplify-Your-Life Day, United Nations: World Wildlife Day, What if Cats and Dogs Had Opposable Thumbs Day, World Birth Defects Day
4. National Backcountry Ski Day, *National Grammar Day, Old Inauguration Day, United Kingdom and Ireland: World Book Day, World Engineering Day for Sustainable Development
5. Crispus Attucks Day (1770), Dress in Blue Day, National Poutine Day, Saint Piran's Day, Shabbat Across American and Canada, World Day of Prayer
6. *Dred Scott day, Ghana: Independence Day, *Michelangelo (1475)
7. Namesake Day, Orthodox Meatfare Sunday
8. Fun Facts About Names Day, International (Working) Women's Day, National Proofreading Day, Syrian Arab Republic: Revolution Day, United Nations: International Women's Day, United States Income Tax Anniversary (1913)
9. *Barbie Day, Belize: Baron Bliss Day, Panic Day, United Kingdom: Commonwealth Day, Unique Names Day
10. Discover What Your Name Means Day, International Bagpipe Day, *Mario Day, National Women and Girls HIV/AIDS Awareness Day, Registered Dietitian Nutritionists Day, *Salvation Army in the US (1880), Sterile Packaging Day, *Telephone Invention (1876), *US Paper Money Issued (1862)
11. Bureau of Indian Affairs Established (1824), Dream 2021 Day, *Johnny Appleseed Day, Key Deer Awareness Day, Lithuania: Restitution of Independence Day, Nametag Day, World Kidney Day
12. *FDR's First Fireside Chat (1933), Gabon: National Day, *Girl Scouts of the USA (1912), Great Blizzard of '88, Lesotho: Moshoeshe's Day, Mauritius: Independence Day, Middle Name Pride Day
13. *Earmuffs Day, Genealogy Day, Good Samaritan Involvement Day, Holy See: National Day, International Fanny Pack Day, National Open an Umbrella Indoors Day, Planet Uranus Discovery Day (1781), Smart and Sexy Day

14. Check Your Batteries Day, Daylight Savings Begins, *Albert Einstein Birthday (1879), England: Mothering Sunday, International Day of Mathematics, Moth-er Day, Pi Day, "10 Most Wanted List" Day (1950)
15. Australia: Canberra Day, Belarus: Constitution Day, Brutus Day, Fill Our Staplers Day, Ides of March, International Day of Action for the Seals, Liberia: J.J. Roberts Day, National Napping Day, National Vo Day, Orthodox Green Monday, True Confessions Day
16. *Black Press Day (1827), Curlew Day, Freedom of Information Day, Goddard Day, *Lips Appreciation Day, National Panda Day, No Selfies Day, US Military Academy Founded (1802)
17. *Campfire USA Day, Evacuation Day, Ireland: National Day, Saint Patrick's Day
18. Absolutely Incredible Kid Day, Aruba: Flag Day, Diesel Day, Forgive Mom and Dad Day, *National Biodiesel Day
19. Certified Nurses Day, *Wyatt Earp (1848), Iran: National Day of Oil, Saint Joseph's Day, Swallows Return to San Juan Capistrano Day, US Standard Time Act (1920)
20. Japan: Vernal Equinox Day, National Quilting Day, Iranian New Year: (Noruz), Naw-Ruz, Ostara, Play the Recorder Day, Proposal Day® (also Sept 22), Save the Florida Panther Day, Snowman Burning, Tunisia: Independence Day, United Nations: French Language Day, *United Nations: International Day of Happiness, Walk in the Sand Day, *Won't You Be My Neighbor Day
21. *Bach Day, England: Care Sunday, *First Round-the-World Balloon Flight (1999), Lesotho: National Tree Planting Day, Memory Day, Namibia: Independence Day, National Healthy Fats Day, South Africa: Human Rights Day, *Twitter Day, *United Nations: International Day for the Elimination of Racial Discrimination, United Nations: International Day of Forests, United Nations: International Nowruz Day, United Nations: World Poetry Day, World Down Syndrome Day
22. As Young As You Feel Day, India: New Year's Day, *International Day of The Seal, *Louis L'Amour Day (1908), Laser Patented Day (1960), *National Goof-off Day, Puerto Rico: Emancipation Day, United Nations: World Day for Water (aka World Water Day)
23. "Big Bertha Paris Gun Day, *Liberty Day, National Agriculture Day, National Puppy Day, National Tamale Day, *Near Miss Day, New Zealand: Otago and Southland Provincial Anniversary, "OK" Day, Pakistan: Republic Day, *United Nations: World Meteorological Day
24. Argentina: National Day of Memory for Truth and Justice, *Education and Sharing Day, Exxon Valdez Oil Spill (1989), *Houdini Day (1874), Philippine Independence, *World Tuberculosis Day
25. *Bed In for Peace Day, *Greece: Independence Day, Maryland Day, National Medal of Honor Day, *Old New Year's Day, Pecan Day, Tolkien Reading Day, United Nations: International Day of Remembrance of The Victims of Slavery and The Transatlantic, United Nations: International Day of Solidarity with Detained and Missing Staff Members
26. Bangladesh: Independence Day, Camp David Accord Day, *Legal Assistants Day, Live Long and Prosper Day, *Make Up Your Own Holiday Day
27. Alaska: Earthquake (1964), Earth Hour, *FDA Approves Viagra Day, Myanmar: Resistance Day, Passover (begins at sundown), *Quirky Country Music Song Titles Day
28. Big Bang Day, Czech Republic: Teachers' Day, European Union: Daylight Saving Time (begins), Palm Sunday, United Kingdom: Summer Time
29. Canada: British North America Act (1867), Central African Republic: Boganda Day, Dow Jones Day, India: Holi, Knights of Columbus Founder's Day, National Mom and Pop Business Owners day, *Niagara Falls Runs Dry (1848), Seward's Day, Taiwan: Youth Day, Texas Loves Children Day

30. Anesthetic Day, *Doctors Day, International Laundry Folding Day, *Pencil Day, The Grass is Always Browner on the Other Side of the Fence Day, Trinidad and Tobago: Spiritual/Shouter Baptist Liberation Day, Vincent Van Gogh Day (1853), World Bipolar Day
31. *Bunsen Burner Day, Cesar Chavez Day, *Eiffel Tower Day (1998), International Hug a Medievalist Day, Little Red Wagon Day, Manatee Appreciation Day, *National "She's Funny That Way" Day, US Virgin Islands: Transfer Day, Whole Grains Sampling Day, World Back-up Day

Holiday Marketing Ideas

International Mirth Month — Let the frivolity begin. You have a whole month to make others smile. Why not email your customers and clients amusing tidbits throughout the month? Make sure you don't add your marketing information every time. Rather, keep it to a minimum. I recommend adding your sell copy every seventh email you send. Lest you forget, humor is healthy, so help them laugh their way to health.

If you are up to the task, you could put together a panel of speakers who could help your audience destress. Life and career coaches would be ideal toward this end. Think about things that make you unhappy and find folks who want to learn how to handle those situations. Then invite them to your International Mirth Month event.

Mar 1 National Pig Day — Start off by using #NationalPigDay to post on social media. Then from there, post pig facts or even graphics that you have branded. These are easy things to do that will take a bit of time and research to accomplish but can be fun and appreciated by the viewers. You'll find one in the Sample Appendix that you can brand and use freely.

Other things you could do are to read a pig story to children or help them make a balloon piggy bank. Alternatively, you could watch a pig movie. *Babe* comes immediately to mind. Then there's always cooking up some pork products and serving them to the homeless. There are a lot of people hurting these days with the impact COVID-19 has had on us, so serving some bar-b-que or bacon would fit the bill nicely. If you put together a team of volunteers to do this, be sure to alert the media. However, if you still want to do something along this line but don't have the wherewithal to do it by yourself, consider contacting your local food bank and volunteering. Interestingly enough, in the 2016 edition of this series you will find the instructions on how to organize a 'virtual food drive'.

Can you name some famous pigs? You'll find a list of a few in the Sample Appendix that you can add to your social media postings or have a contest to see who can name the most. Of course, the prizes should be pig related, including perhaps a bar-b-que restaurant certificate.

Mar 3 Simplify-Your-Life Day — Simplifying your life may mean decluttering or organizing. Either way, today is a terrific opportunity for coaches of all kinds to help others accomplish these lofty goals. Sharing tips on social media or email that will help others to this end is also an easy enough thing to do. Whether it is time management skills or cleaning out your cluttered workspace or home, people need to know how to organize their lives in simple steps. Be sure not to overwhelm them with a complicated process. Why not consider sharing a task each day for the whole week that others can easily accomplish? In the Samples Appendix you will find a few tips that you can use.

May 5 Dress in Blue Day — Dress in Blue Day reminds us of our mission to end this highly preventable disease, colorectal cancer. By wearing blue and raising funds, you bring awareness to this disease — as well as honor all who are impacted by colorectal cancer. So, it's time you pulled together a team and had a fundraising event. This can be done both online and offline. With a little pre-planning you and your team can help bring awareness while raising the funds necessary for both research and care. You can share the graphic in the Samples Appendix either in person or online. Be sure to brand it though for greater recognition of your business.

May 9 Panic Day — Life can become stressful at times with managing your finances, career, family, health, and relationships. Use today to evaluate your priorities and eliminate anything that causes you stress. If you can't eliminate it, find a way to cope, or just take a moment to yourself to scream and then breathe deeply and try again. Organizational, career, and mind, body, soul coaches get together and host a webinar to help your attendees destress their lives. Candle sellers, skincare reps, masseurs, and health care professionals also can find this holiday a good one to help others eliminate the stress they are under. At the very least send out good vibes with tips or graphics in email or social media.

May 13 National Open an Umbrella Indoors Day — Today is all about overcoming your superstitions. They range from throwing salt over your shoulder ... really? ... to stepping on a crack, walking under a ladder, holding your breath as you pass a cemetery (yes, I'm guilty of this one), knocking on wood (okay, so I've done this one too), and many, many more. While it's not quite Friday the 13th, it is time to debunk those things that keep you from being successful. You can be a successful speaker; you can lose that extra pound or two, you can win that triathlon. Whatever it is that is holding you back, it's time to let it go! If you are a myth busting coach, your clients await! Send out a real card or letter to your most loyal clients with a motivational quote. Post some on your social media, twitter the day away, and be sure to open your umbrella indoors!

May 16 Lips Appreciation Day — If you sell makeup this Weird & Wacky holiday is tailor-made for you. If not, a fun thing to do is to have a lip photo contest or just post photos of some famous people's lips and see if your friends can recognize who they are. Okay, you can include an extra photo that includes the nose, that might help if they need a hint. Probably everyone would recognize Jimmy Durante so be sure to include him. If you want, share some facts about lips and celebrate the day by using the hashtag #lipsappreciationday and pucker up!

May 25 Pecan Day — Pecans are my third favorite nut after cashews and macadamias. I keep cinnamon pecans in pantry for adding to salads and snacking. Pecan pie, while I can only eat a ridiculously small piece is a yummy treat, is also a standard for many southern US households. However, roasted pecans are good all by themselves. I am sure you have a favorite pecan dish, unless you have an allergy that is. So, why not visit the Samples Appendix and make a yummy pecan treat to share with your most loyal customers. Package them up and send them off. Whilst a pie might not travel well, you'll find some recipes that you can easily use. Oh, and be sure to include the recipe, your customers and clients will thank you. And they'll think of you every time they use the recipe.

Mar 30 The Grass is Always Browner on the Other Side of the Fence Day—is a chance for you to step back and consider all that you are grateful for in your life and to acknowledge those things that you wish were greener. Make a list with two columns. Begin by celebrating the things on your greener side. Then look at the browner side and consider how you can make those items in your list move over to your greener side. Sharing tips on overcoming challenges that keep you from achieving your lofty goals is a good way to spend your day. During your social media sharing time you might want to use the graphic in the Samples Appendix; after you have branded it of course.

APRIL

Apr 1 – May 9 National Card and Letter Writing Month
Apr 13 – May 12 Ramadan: the Islamic Month of Fasting

Month-Long Holidays

Adopt a Ferret Month, Alcohol Awareness Month, Community Spirit Days, Couple Appreciation Month, Distracted Driving Awareness Month, Global Astronomy Month, Grange Month, Holy Humor Month, Informed Woman Month, International Black Women's History Month, International Customer Loyalty Month, International Twit Award Month, Jazz Appreciation Month, Library Snapshot Day, Mathematics and Statistics Awareness Month, Medical Cannabis Education and Awareness Month, National African American Women's Fitness Month, National Autism Awareness Month, *National Cancer Control Month, *National Child Abuse Prevention Month, *National Donate Life Month, National Exchange Club Child Abuse Prevention Month, National Frog Month, National Heartworm Awareness Month, National Humor Month, National Knuckles Down Month, National Lawn Care Month, National 9-1-1 Education Month, National Pecan Month, National Pest Management Month, National Poetry Month, National Rebuilding Month, *National Sexual Assault Awareness and Prevention Month, National Sexually Transmitted Diseases (STDS) Education and Awareness Month, National Youth Sports Safety Month, Occupational Therapy Month, Pet First Aid Awareness Month, Pharmacists' War on Diabetes, Prevention of Cruelty to Animals Month, Rosacea Awareness Month, School Library Month, Straw Hat Month, Stress Awareness Month, Women's Eye Health and Safety Month, Workplace Conflict Awareness Month, World Landscape Architecture Month, Worldwide Bereaved Spouses Awareness Month

Week-Long Holidays

Apr 1 – 7 Laugh at Work Week, Testicular Cancer Awareness Week
Apr 3 – 12 National Robotics Week
Apr 4 – 10 Hate Week — "Down with Big Brother", National Library Week
Apr 5 – 11 Mule Day
Apr 10 – 11 Just Pray No! Worldwide Weekend of Prayer and Fasting
Apr 11 – 17 National Dog Bite Prevention Week, Pan American Week
Apr 12 – 15 Italy: Bologna Children's Book Fair
Apr 17 – 25 National Park Week (tentative)
Apr 18 – 24 Chemists Celebrate Earth Week, Greece: Dumb Week, National Coin Week, *National Crime Victims' Rights Week, National Volunteer Week, Sky Awareness Week
Apr 19 – 23 Undergraduate Research Week
Apr 22 – 25 Fiddler's Frolics
Apr 24 – 30 World Immunization Week
Apr 25 – May 1 Orthodox Holy Week, Preservation Week

Apr 25 – May 2 Stewardship Week
Apr 29 – May 5 Japan: Golden Week Holidays

Daily Holidays

1. *April Fool's or All Fool's Day, Bulgaria: St Lasarus' Day, Canada: Nunavut Independence (1999), Iran: Islamic Republic Day, Maundy Thursday or Holy Thursday, Mylesday, *Sorry Charlie Day
2. Hans Christian Anderson Day (1805), Argentina: Malvinas Day, Bermuda: Good Friday Kite Flying Day, Good Friday, *Sir Alec Guinness (1914), International Kids' Yoga Day, National Ferret Day, Pascua Florida Day, Ponce de Leon Discovers Florida (1513), *Reconciliation Day, *United Nations: World Autism Awareness Day, US Mint Day
3. Blacks Ruled Eligible to Vote Day (1944), Easter Even, Guinea: Anniversary of the Second Republic, International Pillow Fight Day, *Pony Express Day, National Love Our Children Day, Taiwan: Children's Day, *Tweed Day
4. Maya Angelou Birthday (1928), *Beatles Take Over Music Charts (1964), *Bonza Bottler Day™, Easter Sunday, Flag Act of 1818 Day, Senegal: Independence Day, *United Nations: International Day for Mine Awareness and Assistance in Mine Action, *Vitamin C Day
5. Dyngus Day, Easter Monday, Gold Star Spouses Day, National Deep-Dish Pizza Day
6. Drowsy Driver Awareness Day, National Library Workers Day, North Pole Discovery Day, *Tartan Day, *Teflon Day (1938), Thailand: Chakri Day, Twinkies Day, United Nations: International Day of Sport for Development and Peace
7. *International Beaver Day, International Snailpapers Day, *Metric System Day, National Beer Day (1933), National Bookmobile Day, National Making the First Move Day, *No Housework Day, United Nations: International Day of the Reflection on the Genocide in Rwanda, *United Nations: World Health Day
8. Home Run Record Set by Hank Aaron (1974), International Roma Day, Isreal: Holocaust Day (Yom Hasshoah), Japan: Flower Festival (Hana Matsuri), National Dog Fighting Awareness Day
9. *Civil Rights Bill of 1866 Day, Civil War Ends (1865), *Jenkins Ear Day, Jumbo the Elephant Day, National Former Prisoner of War Recognition Day, Philippines: Araw Ng Kagitingan, Texas Panhandle Tornado Day, Tunisia: Martyrs' Day, *Winston Churchill Day
10. ASPCA Incorporation Day (1866), *Commodore Perry Day, Ireland: Good Friday Peace Agreement in Northern Ireland (1998), National Catch and Release Day, *National Siblings Day, *Salvation Army Founder's Day
11. *Barbershop Quartet Day, Civil Rights Act Day (1968), Costa Rica: Juan Santamaria Day, *International "Louie Louie" Day, National Clean Up Your Pantry Day, National Pet Day, Uganda: Liberation Day, World Parkinson's Day
12. Halifax: Independence Day, *National D.E.A.R. Day (aka Drop Everything and Read), *National Licorice Day, Polio Vaccine Day, Truancy Day, United Nations: International Day of Human Space Flight, *Walk on Your Wild Side Day, Yuri's Night
13. Children's Day in Florida (always the second Tuesday), *Guy Fawkes Day, International Be Kind to Lawyers Day, *Thomas Jefferson Day, South Africa: Family Day, Sri Lanka: Sinhala and Tamil New Year
14. *Children with Alopecia Day, Dictionary Day, Get to Know Your Customers Day (third Thursday of each quarter is set aside to get to know your customers even better), Honduras: Dia de las Americas, India: Vaisakhi, *International Moment of Laughter Day, National Pecan Day, Pan American Day, Pathologists' Assistant Day, World Chagas Day

15. 15. Astronomers Find New Solar System (1999), Boston Marathon and Bombing (2013), Botox Day, First School for Deaf Founded (1817), *Income Tax Pay Day, Israel: Independence Day (Yom Ha'atzma'ut), *McDonald's Day, National High Five Day, *National Take a Wild Guess Day, *National That Sucks Day, Quarterly Estimated Federal Income Tax Payers' Due Date (also Jan 15, Jun 15, and Sep 15, 2021), *Titanic Sinking (1912), World Art Day
16. 16. *Charlie Chaplin Day (1889), Emancipation Day, Get to Know Your Customers Day (third Thursday of each quarter is set aside to get to know your customers even better), National Stress Awareness Day
17. 17. American Samoa: Flag Day, *Blah! Blah! Blah! Day, Herbalist Day, International Haiku Poetry Day, International Raw Milk Cheese Appreciation Day, Record Store Day, Syrian Arab Republic: Independence Day, World Circus Day
18. 18. Canada: Constitution Act of 1982, *International Amateur Radio Day, Paul Revere's Ride Day (1775), *Pet Owners Independence Day, "Third World" Day, World Heritage Day/International Day for Monuments and Sites, Zimbabwe: Independence Day
19. 19. John Parker Day, National Hanging Out Day, Patriots Day in Florida, Sierra Leone: National Holiday, Swaziland: King's Birthday, Uruguay: Landing of the 33 Patriots Day
20. 20. 4/20 Day, United Nations: Chinese Language Day
21. Administrative Professionals Day or Secretary's Day, Aggie Muster Day, Brazil: Tiradentes Day, Indonesia: Kartini Day, Italy: Birthday of Rome, *Kindergarten Day, National Bulldogs are Beautiful Day, Red Baron Day, San Jacinto Day
22. Brazil: Discovery of Brazil Day, Coins Stamped "In God We Trust" Day, *Earth Day, *National Jelly Bean Day, National Teach Children to Save Day, Oklahoma Land Rush Day (1889), Take Our Daughters and Sons to Work® Day (fourth Thursday in April), United Nations: International Mother Earth Day
23. Canada: Newfoundland: Saint George's Day, *Movie Theatre Day, *Public School Day, National English Muffin Day, Saint George Feast Day, William Shakespeare Day (1564), Spain: Book Day and Lover's Day, Turkey: National Sovereignty and Children's Day, United Nations: English Language Day, United Nations: Spanish Language Day, *United Nations: World Book and Copyright Day, World Book Night
24. 24. Armenia: Armenian Martyrs Day, Independent Bookstore Day, Ireland: Easter Rising (1916), Lazarus Saturday, Library of Congress Day, National Rebuilding Day, Pet Tech CPR Day®, World Healing Day, World Tai Chi and Qigong Day, World Veterinary Day
25. 25. Abortion Legalized (1967), Anzac Day, Egypt: Sinai Day, *License Plates Day, Italy: Liberation Day, Orthodox Palm Sunday, Portugal: Liberty Day, Swaziland: National Flag Day, Switzerland: Landsgemeinde, World Malaria Day, World Penguin Day, WWII: East Meets West Day (1945)
26. 26. Audubon Day, *Hug an Australian Day, National Help a Horse Day, National Pretzel Day, *Richter Scale Day, Tanzania: Union Day, United Nations: International Chernobyl Disaster Remembrance Day, United Nations: World Intellectual Property Day
27. 27. Babe Ruth Day (1947), Mantanzas Mule Day, *Morse Code Day, Most Tornadoes in a Day (US), National Little Pampered Dog Day, Netherlands: King's Day, Sierra Leon and Togo: Independence Day, Slovenia: Insurrection Day, South Africa: Freedom Day
28. 28. Biological Clock Gene Discovered (1994), Canada: National Day of Mourning, United Nations: World Day for Safety and Health at Work, Workers Memorial Day
29. 29. Emperor Hirohito Michi-No-Miya Birthday (1901), Japan: Showa Day, *"Peace" Rose Day, Zipper Day (1913)

30. 30. Arbor Day in Arizona, Beltane, *Bugs Bunny Day (1938), Día de los Niños/Día de los Libros, First North America Theatrical Performance Day (1598), International Jazz Day, Louisiana Purchase Day (1803), National Animal Advocacy Day, National Arbor Day, National Hairball Awareness Day, National Honesty Day (Honest Abe Awards), Raisin Day, Organization of American States Founded (1948), Vietnam: Liberation Day, *Walpurgis Night

Holiday Marketing Ideas

Apr 1 – May 9 National Card and Letter Writing Month — This is the time to sit down with the old-fashioned pencil and paper or notecard and pen a note to your customers and clients. Especially now, during the COVID-19 crisis, those real cards and letters will be genuinely appreciated. We are all inundated with emails that are way too easy to merely delete. But physical correspondence is so rare that when you receive something in the snail mail, you are more appreciative of it. You may even keep it around or post it on a place of prominence if the notecard image is inviting.

Apr 2 Reconciliation Day — It's interesting to note that Reconciliation Day follows immediately Sorry Charlie Day on April 1st. Reconnecting with your customers and clients is a superb way to celebrate this Weird & Wacky holiday. So, keep up the letter writing campaign you have begun and add a phone call or two to the mix. If you are a bit leery of the phone, as some people are, you can also send out emails as a way of touching base with them.

Apr 6 Teflon Day — God blessed cooks everywhere with the invention of Teflon! It has a two-fold benefit. First it makes things we cook take less fat which in turn is a boon to our health and second, it makes clean-up a breeze. So, with those thoughts in mind, think healthy tips and quotes and health building webinars.

Alternatively, since clean-up is a breeze, organizational tips or time management skills could be a timely addition to your marketing efforts.

Apr 12 Truancy Day — Attendance matters! For children it's called Truancy, for military it is AWOL, and for employees it is called **fired**, but for business owners it equates to failure. So, I suggest you help others to change their bad habits today. Sharing how they can overcome procrastination or manage their time wisely could be wonderful ways to begin. Tips posted on social media are okay, but a webinar might be a whole lot better. Gather your list of guest speakers and have them share that that they are speaking at your event. This will help build your attendance and since you are the host all marketing pieces will be branded to your business, getting you much wanted publicity.

Apr 17 Blah! Blah! Blah! Day — Today is meant for doing the mundane tasks you have been putting off. Whether that means taking out the trash or cleaning out your inbox, blah, blah, blah, today could end up being a very productive day. Talking about computers, you might want to run a defrag or simply delete old programs you no longer use or fire those troublesome clients who pester you with email after email rather than consolidating their messages. In that vein, why not consider sharing some tips on how to be more productive? Social media is a good place to start, but perhaps you should consider sending a quick email to your customers wishing them a Happy Blah! Blah! Blah! Day. Make it personal so they know it's not a spam email and make them smile with the branded graphic you include. You'll find one in the Samples Appendix that you can feel free to use to your hearts content.

Apr 23 Public School Day — COVID-19 has had a huge impact on our public school system. While many parents are homeschooling, others don't have that option and are sending their kids back to the classroom environment. Those brave few who serve them are also at risk, whether they be janitors, teachers, bus drivers, or administrators they all need our continued support. Your support of them all could include fundraising to supply the tools that the teachers themselves often must provide. While you are at it, be sure to alert the media. You never know when they will turn their microphone and camera your way.

If you want something easy to do, you can always use the graphic I designed which you will find in the Samples Appendix.

Apr 30 Raisin Day — Here's a healthy snack that comes in a variety of colors. No matter what your favorite, it's hard to disagree with the fact that these delectable treats are used in almost everything. From muesli to oatmeal raisin cookies, these tasty treats are both healthy and delicious. So, how do you turn Raisin Day into a marketing event? Easy. Look at the benefits and uses and you will come to the same conclusion I have. Recipe swap day is in order! Okay, I hear you, how about making health and nutrition your focus?

According to OrganicFacts.net, some of the top benefits of raisins include:
- Preventing cancer with antioxidants
- Reducing blood pressure
- Relieving constipation due to their high fiber content
- Treating erectile disfunction
- Helping in treating anemia and fever
- Helping build strong bones
- Helping keep acidosis in check
- Promoting good cardia health
- Aiding in healthy weight gain
- Modulating blood sugar in diabetics
- Protecting eyes and teeth against infection

With this information in hand, you could easily put together a graphic or some tips you can share on social media.

MAY

May 1–31 Philippines: Santacruzan
May 11–22 Cannes Film Festival
May 31–Sep 6 National Marina Days

Month-Long Holidays

American Cheese Month, *Asian American and Pacific Islander Heritage Month, Asthma Awareness Month, Celiac Disease Awareness Month, College Students with Disabilities Recognition Month, Fibromyalgia Education and Awareness Month, Gardening for Wildlife Month, Gifts from the Garden Month, Haitian Heritage Month, Heal the Children Month, Huntington's Disease Awareness Month, International Mediterranean Diet Month, International Victorious Woman Month, *Jewish American Heritage Month, Law Enforcement Appreciation Month In Florida, Mental Health Month, Motorcycle Safety Month, Mystery Month, National Allergy/Asthma Awareness Month, National Arthritis Awareness Month, National Barbecue Month, National Bike Month, National Foster Care Month, National Hamburger Month, National Hepatitis Awareness Month, National Meditation Month, National Military Appreciation Month, National Osteoporosis Month, National Physical Fitness and Sports Month, National Preservation Month, National Read to Your Baby Bump Month, National Salad Month, National Vinegar Month, *Older Americans Month, React Month, Save Your Tooth Month, Skin Cancer Awareness Month, Spiritual Literacy Month, Strike Out Strokes Month, Ultraviolet Awareness Month, Women's Health Care Month, Young Achievers/Leaders of Tomorrow Month

Week-Long Holidays

May 1–7 Choose Privacy Week
May 2–8 Be Kind to Animals Week®, National Family Week, National Hug Holiday Week, National Hurricane Preparedness Week, National Pet Week, National Small Business Week, Update Your References Week
May 3–7 Teacher Appreciation Week
May 6–12 National Nurses Week
May 9–15 National Police Week, Salute to 35+ Moms Week
May 10–14 National Etiquette Week
May 14–15 Fishing Has No Boundaries Days
May 10–16 National Stuttering Awareness Week, Tick Awareness Week, Work at Home Moms Week
May 16–21 National Foul Ball Week
May 16–22 International New Friends Old Friends Week, National Transportation Week, National Unicycle Week, World Trade Week
May 22–28 National Safe Boating Week
May 30–Jun 5 National African Violet Week

Daily Holidays

1. *Amtrak, Batman Day, Batman Debut Anniversary (1939), Free Comic Book Day, Great Britain Formed Day (1707), Hug Your Cat Day, *Keep Kids Alive—Drive 25® Day, Kentucky Derby, Labor Day, *Law Day, *Lei Day, *Loyalty Day, *May Day, May One Day, Mother Goose Day, National Auctioneers Day, National Bubba Day, National Fancy Hat Lunch Day, National Fitness 0Day, National Learn to Ride a Bike Day, *New Home Owners Day, Russia: International Labor Day, *School Principals' Day
2. King James Bible Published Day, Motorcycle Mass and Blessing of the Bikes, National Infertility Survival® Day, Orthodox Easter Sunday or Pascha, Red Baron Day, Robert's Rules Day, United Nations: World Tuna Day
3. Dow Jones Tops 11,000 Day (1999), *Garden Meditation Day, Japan: Constitution Memorial Day, Labor Day Observed, *Lumpy Rug Day, Melanoma Monday, Mexico: Day of the Holy Cross, National Public Radio Day, National Specially-Abled Pets Day, *National Two Different Colored Shoes Day, Poland: Constitution Day (Swieto Trzeciego Maja), *United Nations: World Press Freedom Day
4. China: Youth Day, Curaçao: Memorial Day, Japan: Greenery Day, National Teacher Day, Rhode Island: Independence Day, *Star Wars Day
5. African World Heritage Day, AMA Founded Day (1847), *Bonza Bottler Day™, *Cartoonists Day, *Cinco de Mayo, Ethiopia: Patriots Victory Day, International Day of the Midwife, Japan and South Korea: Children's Day, National Bike to School Day, Netherlands: Liberation Day, World Asthma Day, World Portuguese Language Day
6. International Management Accounting Day, *Joseph Brackett Day, National Day of Prayer, National Day of Reason, *No Diet Day, *No Homework Day, Orson Wells Day (1915)
7. Beaufort Scale Day, Cystinosis Awareness Day, Dow Jones Tops 15000 (2013), El Salvador: Day of the Soldier, Military Spouse Appreciation Day
8. Czech Republic: Liberation Day, England: Heston Furry dance/Flora Day, France: Victory Day, International Migratory Bird Day, Italy: Giro D'Italia, Jamestown Day, Letter Carriers' "Stamp Out Hunger" Food Drive, National Train Day, Netherlands: National Windmill Day, *No Socks Day, Slovakia: Liberation Day, Stay Up All Night Night, *United Nations: Time of Remembrance and Reconciliation WWII (8–9), United Nations: World Migratory Bird Day, *V E Day (1945), World Fair Trade Day,*World Red Cross Red Crescent Day
9. European Union Founded (1950), Mother's Day, Mother's Day at the Wall, Rogation Sunday, Rural Life Sunday, Russia: Victory Day, Taiwan: Birthday of Buddha, Uzbekistan: Day or Memory and Honor
10. Golden Spike Driving Day (1758), Israel: Jerusalem Day (Yom Yerushalayim), Micronesia: Constitution Day, World Lupus Day
11. Salvador Dali Day, *Eat What You Want Day
12. Donate a Day's Wages to Charity Day, *Limerick Day, Native American Rights Recognized Anniversary (1879), National Nightshift Workers Day, National Receptionists Day, National School Nurse Day, National Third Shift Workers Day, Florence Nightingale Day, *Odometer Day
13. Ascension Day, Electric Razor Day, National Hummus Day
14. Fahrenheit Day, Fintastic Friday: Giving Sharks a Voice, *Lewis and Clark Expedition Sets Out Day (1804), Smallpox Vaccine Discovery (1796), *The Stars and Stripes Forever Day, *Underground America Day, WAAC Day (1942)

15. Fishing Has No Boundaries Day, Flight Attendant Day, International Learn to Swim Day, Japan: Aoi Matsuri (Hollyhock Festival), Mexico: San Isidro Day, Nakba Day, National Sliders Day, *Nylon Stockings Day, Paraguay: Independence Day, *Peace Officer Memorial Day, *United Nations: International Day of Families
16. Armed Forces Day, *Academy Awards Day (1929), *Biographer's Day, First Woman to Climb Mt. Everest Day (1975), International Day of Light, Peabody Day, Preakness Stakes, Ride a Unicycle Day, Shavout (begins at sundown)
17. Brown vs. Board of Education (1954), *First Kentucky Derby Day (1875), *Same-Sex Marriages Day (2004), Norway: Constitution Day, *United Nations: World Telecommunications and Information Society Day
18. Haiti: Flag and University Day, *International Museum Day, Uruguay: Battle of Las Piedras Day, *Visit Your Relatives Day
19. *Boys Club Day, China: Birth of Lord Buddha, Dark Day in New England, Hepatitis Testing Day, Ho Chi Minh Birthday (1890), Turkey: Youth and Sports Day
20. *Amelia Earhart Atlantic Crossing Day (1932), Cameroon: National Holiday, East Timor: Anniversary of Independence, *Eliza Doolittle Day, Lindbergh Flight (1927), Mecklenburg Day, United Nations: World Bee Day, *Weights and Measures Day, World Aiarthritis Day
21. *American Red Cross Founder's Day, Chile: Battle of Iquique Day, Endangered Species Day, *I Need a Patch for That Day, International Virtual Assistants Day, National Bike to Work Day, National Defense Transportation Day, National Pizza Party Day, *National Wait Staff Day, Teacher's Day in Florida, *United Nations: World Day for Cultural Diversity for Dialogue and Development
22. *National Maritime Day, Sri Lanka: National Heroes Day, *United Nations: International Day for Biological Diversity, US Colored Troops Founders Day, World Goth Day, Yemen: National Day
23. *Bonnie and Clyde Death (1934), Declaration of the Bab, *International World Turtle Day®, Morocco: National Day, National Best Friend-In-Law Day, New York Public Library Day, Pentecost, Sweden: Linnaeus Day, United Nations: International Day to End Obstetric Fistula, WhitSunday
24. Belize: Commonwealth Day, Brooklyn Bridge Open (1883), *Brother's Day, Bulgaria: Culture Day, Canada: Victory Day, England: Dicing for Bibles, Eritrea: Independence Day, International Tiara Day, *Morse Code Day, Queen Victory Day, WhitMonday
25. African Freedom Day, Argentina: Revolution Day, *Ralph Waldo Emerson Birthday (1803), Germany: Waldchestag (Forest Day), *Greatest Day in Track and Field: Jessie Owens' Day, Jordan: Independence Day, Memorial Day, *National Missing Children's Day, *National Tap Dance Day, Poetry Day in Florida, *Towel Day, United Nations: Week of Solidarity with Peoples of Non-Self-Governing Territories
26. Australia: Sorry Day, Georgia: Independence Day, John Wayne (1907), World Lindy Hop Day, World Otter Day
27. First Flight into the Stratosphere (1931), First Running of the Preakness, *Golden Gate Bridge Day
28. *Amnesty International Founded (1961), Ascension of Baha'u'llah, Azerbaijan: Day of the Republic, Ethiopia and Nepal: National Day, *Sierra Club Day, *Slugs Return from Capistrano Day
29. *Amnesty for Southern Rebels Day, *Mount Everest Summit Reached (1953), *United Nations: International Day of United Nations Peacekeepers

30. Fabergé Day, *First American Daily Newspaper Published (1783), Haiti: Mother's Day, *Indianapolis 500 (1911), *Loomis Day, Memorial Day (Traditional), Trinidad and Tobago: Indian Arrival Day, Trinity Sunday
31. *Copyright Law Passed (1970), Johnstown Flood Day, Memorial Day, Prayer for Peace Memorial Day, *United Nations: World No-Tobacco Day, *Walt Whitman Day, *What You Think Upon Grows Day

Holiday Marketing Ideas

National Preservation Month—This month we have a lot of choices on how to celebrate. Things like shopping in your local Main Street downtown historical areas and dining out at a historical building which has been repurposed as a restaurant. While you are shopping in your local historic district, snap a photo and share it on your favorite social media and use the hashtag #ThisPlaceMatters. If you take the latter to your marketing heart, find out where there is one in your best, most loyal client's locale and send them gift certificates to dine there.

If you really want to get your hands dirty, join a restoration project. The more you involve yourself in your community, the more people will know about you and what you do. We are naturally curious creatures, and I am positive someone will ask you what you do. Word will get around, and you might just end up getting some new clients.

May 1 National Fancy Hat Lunch Day—Hats have been worn for many millennia, and even longer than that. So, it is fitting to celebrate the chapeaux. Whether it is a fancy baseball cap, or a fascinator today is the day to show it off. And don't forget that today only it is appropriate to wear your hat whilst you dine with your clients and friends. Purple and Red Hat ladies, this is your day to shine. If you aren't a member, you can always post photos on the web of you and your team in their favorite millinery creation.

As a point of interest, you could also post tips on how to wear your topper with etiquette and panache. You'll find a list of etiquette instructions in the Samples Appendix. Use them to create tips and graphics as you wish your crowd a very happy National Fancy Hat Lunch Day.

May 7 Military Spouse Appreciation Day—It seems like those who serve our country are the ones we focus on most when we think of the military. We have all kinds of projects for the men and women who serve, but those left behind to wait and wonder are hardly ever even given a moment's thought. So, today we turn that around and focus on the fathers and mothers who remain at home caring for the home and family to await their soldier's return.

So, as you consider the ways you will celebrate today while increasing your marketing reach why not do something that will garner media attention? Something as simple as putting together a team of volunteers to pass out a flower to each of them or even offering to mind the children so they can take a well needed break from the mundane. Their break could be taking a bubble bath or going out for the day. Talking about bubble bath, why not consider wrapping a small bottle with your brand wrapper and giving that to them instead of or along with the flower. Another offering could be the bubble bath and a scented candle. Those are a bit more expensive, so it may not work with your budget, but there's always donors and sponsors like *Military Spouses Magazine* or March of Dimes who could help fund your project. And if you are of those fortunate few, your logo can be included on all media promotional material.

If you prefer to do something you can accomplish by yourself, get a list of military spouses and send them a notecard to show you care. The place to start looking for those folks is to look at the list of military spouse-owned businesses. You'll find the link in the Resources.

May 11 Eat What You Want Day — It's time to step away from your healthy food and go directly to your cravings; no diets allowed. Indulge in something you have resisted that you love. That's the theme of the day. If you are a cook, or own a restaurant, you could offer a coupon or discount to your customers, so that they can treat themselves to something they might not have ordered otherwise. Or, how about giving a gift certificate to a restaurant chain to your very best customers if you aren't a restaurateur or chef? At least a social media graphic is in order, wouldn't you say?

May 12 Odometer Day — An odometer tells you how far you've gone. Therefore, on Odometer Day the thing to do is to step back and evaluate that plan you wrote in January. You did update your business and marketing plan for the year, right? Well, if you didn't it is time to write it now. In that vein helping others learn how to write a business and/or marketing plan and how to evaluate their progress and decide if they need to adjust to a different route is the thing to do. So, join with some speakers who know about these subjects and plan an event worth marketing or offer to speak at someone else's event. Be sure you choose speakers who have a large target audience so that your efforts won't be in vain. They will let their tribe know that they are speaking at your event and that will mean more people will attend. In the Appendix I have put together an event flyer that you can use or gain inspiration from.

May 15 International Learn to Swim Day — I recently read that there are benefits to learning how to swim that I never knew about before. As an example, did you know that children who were taught to swim by age 5 experienced several cognitive and physical advantages over children who did not know how to swim. They were also more advanced in mathematics, counting, language, and following instructions. In the Samples Appendix you'll find a social media graphic I was inspired by poolscouts.com's 2018 graphic to recreate for you.

However, looking at this Weird & Wacky holiday for marketing inspiration I begin by pondering the safety of learning this skill, you won't drown, and the physical exercise you get as you participate in this sport. Now, if we add the additional cognitive and physical advantages mentioned above, you have several ways to help others, especially if you are an educator or sports trainer.

Nevertheless, those of us who are neither will have to think more about brain training and maybe twist it to mean you can focus on an event that teaches others how to prevent or lessen their chance of getting Alzheimer's or improve their focus to stay on track in their businesses. When you partner with speakers who thoroughly know these subjects, people will listen.

JUNE

Jun 1 – Jul 4 Fireworks Safety Months
Jun 26 – Oct 31 Great American Campout
Jun 27 – Jul 19 Tour de France

Month-Long Holidays

Adopt-A-Shelter-Cat Month, *African American Music Appreciation Month, Alzheimer's and Brain Awareness Month, Audiobook Appreciation Month, Canada: National Indigenous History Month, Cancer From the Sun Month, *Caribbean American Heritage Month, Cataract Awareness Month, Child Vision Awareness Month, Dementia Care Professionals Month, Effective Communications Month, Entrepreneurs "Do It Yourself" Marketing Month, Gay and Lesbian Pride Month, *Great Outdoors Month, International Men's Month, International Surf Music Month, June Dairy Month, Men's Health Education and Awareness Month, Migraine and Headache Awareness Month, National Aphasia Awareness Month, National Bathroom Reading Month, National Candy Month, National Caribbean American Heritage Month, National Foster a Pet Month, National Iced Tea Month, *National Oceans Month, National Pollinator Month, National Rivers Month, National Rose Month, National Safety Month, National Soul Food Month, Outdoor Marketing Month, Perennial Gardening Month, Pharmacists Declare War on Alcoholism Month, PTSD Awareness Month, Rainbow Book Month™, Rebuild Your Life Month, Skyscraper Month, Student Safety Month, World Roller Coaster Appreciation Month, National Zoo and Aquarium Month

Week-Long Holidays

Jun 5 – 12 International Clothesline Week
Jun 6 – 12 Bed Bug Awareness Week, National Business Etiquette Week
Jun 13 – 19 National Flag Week
Jun 13 – 20 National Hermit Week
Jun 14 – 20 Meet a Mate Week
Jun 17 – 20 US Open
Jun 20 – 26 Greencare for Troops Awareness Week, Lightning Safety Awareness Week
Jun 21 – 27 National Pollinator Week
Jun 25 – 26 Little Bighorn Days
Jun 26 – 27 ARRL Field Day

Daily Holidays

1. Baby Boomers Recognition Day, China: International Children's Day, *Heimlich Maneuver Day, Samoa: Independence Day, Say Something Nice Day, Superman Day, United Nations: Global Day of Parents

2. Bhutan: Coronation Day, Global Running Day, Italy: Republic Day, Saint Erasmus Day, United Kingdom: Coronation Day, *Yell Fudge at the Cobras in North America Day (Don't laugh, I haven't seen any lately!)
3. *Chimborazo Day, Corpus Christi, United Nations: World Bicycle Day, Zoot Suit Riots Anniversary (1943)
4. Bahamas: Labor Day, China: Tiananmen Square Massacre (1989), Finland: Flag Day, First Free Flight by a Woman (1784), National Donut Day, National Gun Violence Awareness Day, Pulitzer Prize Day (1917), Tonga: Emancipation Day, *United Nations: International Day of Innocent Children Victims of Aggression Day
5. *AIDS First Noted (1981), *Apple II (1977), Belmont Stakes, Denmark: Constitution Day, First Balloon Flight (1783), HIV Long-term Survivors Awareness Day, Iran: Fifteenth of Khordad, National Trails Day, *United Nations: World Environment Day
6. *Bonza Bottler Day™, Celebration of the Arts Day, Corpus Christi US (observed), *D–Day (1944), *Drive in Movie Day (1933), Japan: Day of the Rice God, Korea: Memorial Day, National Cancer Survivors Day, National Yo-Yo Day, Prop 13 Day (1978), *SEC Day (1934), Sweden: National Day, United Nations: Russian Language Day, YMCA Day
7. *(Daniel) Boone Day, Mackintosh Day, Malta: National Day, Supreme Court Strikes Down Connecticut Law Banning Contraception (1965)
8. American Heroine Woman Rewarded (1697), National Call Your Doctor Day, *United Nations: World Ocean Day, *Upsy Daisy Day, World Oceans Day
9. *Donald Duck Day, International Archives Day
10. *AA Day (1935), Congo: Brazzaville (Day of National Reconciliation), Jordan: Great Arab Revolt and Army Day, National Ballpoint Pen Day, National Iced Tea Day, Orthodox Ascension Day, Portugal: Day of Portugal, US Mint Day
11. Jacques Cousteau (1910), *King Kamehameha Day (First Hawaiian King), Libya: Evacuation Day, National Cotton Candy Day
12. *Baseball's First Perfect Game (1880), First Man-Powered Flight Across English Channel (1979), Loving v. Virginia Day (1967), Orlando Nightclub Massacre (2016), Paraguay: Peace with Bolivia Day, Philippines: Independence Day, Russia: Russia Day, *"Tear Down This Wall" Day, United Nations: World Day Against Child Labor
13. Children's Day in Massachusetts, Children's Sunday, Race Unity Day, United Nations: International Albinism Awareness Day
14. Alzheimer Day, Family History Day, First Nonstop Transatlantic Flight (1919), First US Breach of Promise Day, *Flag Day, Japan: Rice Planting Festival, Malawi: Freedom Day, UNIVAC Computer Day, US Army Day, World Blood Donor Day
15. *Magna Carta Day (1215), National Prune Day, Native American Citizenship Day, *Nature Photography Day, Quarterly Estimated Federal Income Tax Payers' Due Date (also Jan 15, Apr 15, and Sep 15, 2021), United Nations: World Elder Abuse Awareness Day
16. *Bloomsday, First Roller Coaster Opens Day (1884), House Divided Speech (1858), *Ladies' Day (Baseball), South Africa: Youth Day
17. Bunker Hill Day, Iceland: Independence Day, Recess at Work Day, South Africa Repeals Last Apartheid Law (1991), *United Nations: World Day to Combat Desertification and Drought
18. Battle of Waterloo Day, Egypt: Evacuation Day, Seychelles: Constitution Day, United Nations: Sustainable Gastronomy Day, Work@Home Father's Day

19. Belmont Stakes Day, Lou Gehrig Day, *Juneteenth, Longest Dam Race Day, Texas: Emancipation Day, United Nations: International Day for the Elimination of Sexual Violence in Conflict, Uruguay: Artigas Day, "War is Hell" Day (1879), World Juggling Day, *World Sauntering Day
20. Anne and Samantha Day (also Dec 21), Argentina: Flag Day, Father's Day, *First Doctor of Science Earned by a Woman Day (1895), Midsummer Day/Eve, Orthodox Pentecost, *United Nations: World Refugee Day
21. Canada: Discover Day (Newfoundland and Labrador), Canada: National Indigenous Peoples Day, Go Skateboarding Day, Greenland: National Holiday, National Energy Shopping Day, United Nations: International Day of Yoga, World Music Day/Fête de la Musique
22. Croatia: Antifascist Struggle Day, Malta: Mnarja, National Columnists' Day, Stupid Guy Thing Day, United Kingdom: National Windrush Day, US Department of Justice (1870)
23. Estonia: Victory Day, *Let It Go Day, Luxembourg: National Holiday, Runner's Selfie Day, United Nations: International Widows Day, United Nations: Public Service Day
24. Canada: Saint John the Baptiste Day, *Celebration of the Senses Day, China: Macau Day, "Flying Saucer" Day, Latvia: John's Day, National Handshake Day, Peru: Countryman's Day, Saint John the Baptist Day, Venezuela: Battle of Carabobo Day
25. Bhutan: National Day, Korea: Tano Day, Mozambique: Independence Day, National Food Truck Day, Slovenia: National Day, Supreme Court Ruling Day (Bans School Prayer, Upholds Rights to Die), Take Your Dog to Work Day˚, Two Yugoslav Republics Declare Independence (1991), United Nations: Day of the Seafarer
26. *Barcode Day, CN Tower Day (1976), Federal Credit Union Act (1934), Human Genome Mapped (2000), Madagascar: Independence Day, Saint Lawrence Seaway Dedication (1959), Supreme Court Strikes Down Defense of Marriage Act (2013), United Nations Charter Signing (1945), *United Nations: International Day Against Drug Abuse and Illicit Trafficking, *United Nations: International Day in Support of Victims of Torture
27. *Decide to be Married Day, Djibouti: Independence Day, *Happy Birthday to "Happy Birthday to You" Day, Industrial Workers of the World Day, Log Cabin Day, *National HIV Testing Day, PTSD Awareness Day, United Nations: Micro-, Small-, and Medium-Sized Enterprises Day
28. International Lightning Safety Day, Monday Holiday Law (1968), Treaty of Versailles (1919)
29. *Death Penalty Ban Day, Interstate Highway System Born (1956), Saint Peter and Paul Day, Saint Peter's Day, Seychelles: Independence Day, United Nations: International Day of the Tropics
30. Asteroid Day, Britain Cedes Claim to Hong Kong (1997), Charles Blondin's Conquest of Niagara Falls (1859), Congo: Independence Day, Gone with the Wind Published (1936), Guatemala: Armed Forces Day, *Leap Second Adjustment Time Day, *NOW (National Organization of Women) Founded (1966), Sudan: Revolution Day

Holiday Marketing Ideas

National Bathroom Reading Month — If you are an author or have anything to do with publishing you really should consider celebrating this month-long Weird & Wacky holiday. Others who might dare to consider this as an excuse to market their business would do well to recommend to their customers and clients a reading list that will help them develop as business owners and people. Surely you can recommend a book or two. Why not post a reading list on your website? Here's an extra tip: if you become an Amazon Affiliate you can even make a small commission on the sales from your website. So, you see, it's not always about having to market, just set up a store on your website and reap the rewards. Of course, you'll still have to let folks know you have added a shop to your website.

Jun 6 National Yo-Yo Day—Celebrating this day with yo-yo demonstrations, prizes, and treats at an event you host is a very fun way to commemorate this day. Children of all ages love Yo-Yos and learning the special techniques that make Yo-Yoing entertaining will add to your enjoyment. Truly, these events are best done in person, but with COVID-19 perhaps still an issue, you might want to do videos and post them on your YouTube channel or website. Then at your online event, you can merely play the training videos in which you have placed your logo in the corner. If you use YouTube, your traffic will be better than if you use your own website, due to the mere numbers that YouTube offers, but you give them your SEO (Search Engine Optimization) though. So, you have to decide which is more important to you, traffic or SEO.

Okay, so now that you have this idea, let's take it another step. Consider all the things we yo-yo about. Our weight & nutrition, think health seminars or our business focus, think procrastination and organization, as well as time management skills. Keep thinking and I'm sure you can come up with more ideas. Oh, and while you are creating your event flyers feel free to use the above graphic that I created in your marketing pieces.

Jun 12 "Tear Down This Wall" Day—On the same vein as Yo-Yo Day, things that get in your way of succeeding in your endeavors should be the subject de jour today. Procrastination and fear are the top two in my book. While fear is a good thing, it can freeze you in your tracks if you allow it to do so. So, helping others overcome their debilitating non-action can spur them on to even greater success and you should definitely consider hosting such an event. However, those are not the only subjects that could be the topic of your event. Religious bias, and injustice of all kinds, especially in this climate, could be tackled if you are up to it. Then there are simply bad habits such as overeating, swearing, and spending too much time playing games or on social media. All these are up for contention in your event roster list.

For those of you who aren't into event marketing— if you aren't you truly might need to consider adding it to your marketing toolkit—there's always the tried and true social media posts and graphics. I have created one and placed it in the usual place for you to brand to your business and freely use.

Jun 15 National Prune Day—Is it just a coincidence or did National Prune Day end up on the same day that your Quarterly Taxes are due? *wink* When thinking of the lowly prune consider its qualities, it is small and sweet, and has many uses including health benefits. So, perhaps focus on the healthy benefits of prunes. You can post tips that include them on social media. You'll find a short list of a few in the Samples Appendix.

Then there's also, the act of pruning. Now that one I think would work well too. Pruning your old Facebook friends who no longer interact with you or are bothersome and culling your newsletter subscriptions are both good starts. To this end you'll find a social media graphic as well that you can use. You know where. *wink*

Whether you chose to hold a webinar or just post tips and graphics be sure you don't just give out the advice but take it too.

Jun 27 United Nations: Micro-, Small-, and Medium-Sized Enterprises Day—Oh my! You have got to sit up and take notice of this Weird & Wacky holiday. Not only is it officially declared by the UN, but it also celebrates all the Mom and Pop businesses throughout the world. So, encourage everyone you know to take the day away from shopping the big multinationals firms and shop at the more unique stores. One way to do that is to put together a list of your friends and colleagues who own smaller sized businesses and create a webpage with all their shops listed along with their URLs. You can offer a discount or coupon code if you like. But, when you join forces with other small business owners and everyone shares the link to the website, you can make an impact that will be felt by those conglomerates!

JULY

Jul 2 – 25 Tour de France
Jul 3 – Aug 11 Dog Days
Jul 3 – Aug 15 Air Conditioning Appreciation Days
Jul 30 — Aug 8 World Police and Fire Games 2021

Month-Long Holidays

Alopecia Month for Women, International, Bioterrorism/Disaster Education and Awareness Month, Cell Phone Courtesy Month, Herbal/Prescription Interaction Awareness Month, National Deli Salad Month, National "Doghouse Repairs" Month, National Grilling Month, National Horseradish Month, National Hot Dog Month, National Ice Cream Month, National Make a Difference to Children Month, National Minority Mental Health Awareness Month, National Park and Recreation Month, National Watermelon Month, Sarcoma Awareness Month, Smart Irrigation Month, Women's Motorcycle Month, Worldwide Bereaved Parents Awareness Month

Week-Long Holidays

Jul 4 – 10 Be Nice to Jersey Week
Jul 10 – 11 Sodbuster Days
Jul 11 – 17 National Farrier's Week, Sports Cliché Week
Jul 17 – 25 National Moth Week
Jul 18 – 24 Captive Nations Week
Jul 18 – 25 Restless Leg Syndrome (RLS) Education and Awareness Week
Jul 22 – 24 Sloppy Joe's Hemmingway® Look-alike Contest
Jul 22 – 25 Comic–Con International
Jul 23 – 25 Annie Oakley Days, Arcadia Daze
Jul 23 – 25 Japan: Soma No Umaoi (Wild Horse Chasing)
Jul 25 – 31 Women in Baseball Week
Jul 31 – Aug 1 Moby Dick Marathon
Jul 31 – Aug 7 England Cowes Week

Daily Holidays

1. Botswana: Sir Seretse Khama Day, Burundi: Independence Day, Canada: Canada Day, Caribbean Day or Caricom Day, China: Half-year Day, *First Photographs Used in Newspaper Report (1848), *First Scheduled Television Broadcast (1941), Ghana: Republic Day, Medicare Day, Postage Stamp Day, Resolution Renewal Day, Rwanda: Independence Day, Somalia Democratic Republic: National Day, Suriname: Liberation Day, *Zip Code Day, Zoo Day

2. Amelia Earhart Disappears (1937), *Civil Rights Day, *Constitution Day (USA), Declaration of Independence Resolution (1776), First Solo Round-the-World Balloon Flight (2002), Halfway Point Day
3. Air-conditioning Appreciation Days, Belarus: Independence Day, *Compliment Your Mirror Day, Quebec Founded (1608), *Stay Out of the Sun Day, United Nations: International Day of Cooperative
4. *America the Beautiful Day, Declaration of Independence Signing (1776), *Fourth of July or Independence Day, *Anne Landers (1918), *Lou Gehrig Day (1939), Philippines: Fil-American Friendship Day
5. Algeria: Independence Day, *Bikini Day, Cape Verde: National Day, Caribbean Day or Caricom Day, Earth at Aphelion Day, *National Labor Relations Day, Slovakia: Saint Cyril and Methodius Day, Venezuela: Independence Day, Zambia: Heroes Day
6. Comoros: Independence Day, Czech Republic: Commemoration Day of Burning of John Hus, First Airship Crossing of the Atlantic (1919), First Successful Antirabies Inoculation (1885), Isle of Man: Tynwald Day, Lithuania: Day of Statehood, Luxembourg: Ettelbruck Remembrance Day, Malawi: Republic Day, Republican Party Day, *Take Your Webmaster to Lunch Day, Zambia: Unity Day
7. *Bonza Bottler Day™, *Father–Daughter Take a Walk Together Day, Japan: Tanabata (Star Festival), Solomon Islands: Independence Day, Spain: Running of the Bulls, Tanzania: Saba Saba Day
8. Aspinwall Crosses US on Horseback (1911), *SCUD Day (Savor the Comic, Unplug the Drama)
9. Argentina: Independence Day, First Open-Heart Surgery Day (1893), Highest Tsunami in Recorded History Day (1958), Martyrdom of the Bab, Morocco: Youth Day, National Motorcycle Day, South Sudan: Independence Day
10. Bahamas: Independence Day, Bald is In Day, Carver Day, *Clerihew Day, *Don't Step on a Bee Day, Stone House Day
11. Bowdler's Day, *Day of the Five Billion, Make Your Own Sundae Day, Mongolia: Naadam National Holiday, *United Nations: World Population Day
12. Different Colored Eyes Day, Family Feud Day (1976), India: Ratha Yatra, International Town Criers Day, Kiribati: Independence Day, National Pecan Pie Day, Northern Ireland: Orangemen's Day
13. *Embrace Your Geekness Day, France: Night Watch (La Retraite Aux Flambeaux, *Gruntled Workers Day, "Live Aid" Day, National Beef Tallow Day, National Nitrogen Ice Cream Day, Republic of Montenegro: National Day, World Cup Day (1930)
14. England: Birmingham Riots Day (1791), France: Night Watch (Bastille Day)
15. Get to Know Your Customers Day (third Thursday of each quarter is set aside to get to know your customers even better), Japan: Bon (Feast of Lanterns), *Rembrandt Day, Saint Swithin's Day, United Nations: World Youth Skills Day
16. Amazon Incorporated (1995), Atomic Bomb Test Day (1945), Boliva: La Paz Day, Get to Know Your Customers Day (third Thursday of each quarter is set aside to get to know your customers even better)
17. Astor Day, Disneyland Opened (1955), Korea: Constitution Day, Minimum Legal Drinking Age at 21 Day, National Bride Sale Day, National Woodie Wagon Day, Puerto Rico: Muñoz–Rivera Day, Toss Away the "Could Haves" and "Should Haves" Day, Women's Dive Day, World Emoji Day, "Wrong Way" Corrigan Day (1938)

18. Mandela Day, National Ice Cream Day, Red Skelton Day (1913), Tisha B'av or Fast of Ab, United Nations: Nelson Mandela International Day, Uruguay: Constitution Day
19. Elvis Presley First Single Day, Japan: Marine Day, *Art Linkletter (1912), National Get Out of the Doghouse Day, Nicaragua: National Liberation Day, Saint Vincent de Paul Day
20. Columbia: Independence Day, Genva Accords (1954), Riot Act Day, *Special Olympics Day, United Nations: World Chess Day
21. Belgium: Independence Day, Guam: Liberation Day, *Hemingway Day (1899), Lowest Recorded Temperature Day (1983), No Pet Store Puppies Day, Take Your Poet to Work Day
22. John Dillinger Day, *Pied Piper Day, *Rat-catchers Day, *Spooner's (Spoonerism) Day
23. Egypt: Revolution Day, *Hot Enough for Ya Day
24. *Cousins Day, Amelia Earhart Day, National Day of the Cowboy, *National Drive-Thru Day, Pioneer Day
25. Auntie's Day®, Costa Rica: Guanacast Day, First Airplane Crossing of English Channel (1909), Puerto Rico: Constitution Day, Spain: Saint James Day, Tunisia: Republic Day
26. Americans with Disabilities Day, Armed Forces Unified (1947), Cuba: National Day (1953), Curaçao Day, International Day for the Conservation of the Mangrove Ecosystem, Liberia and Maldives: Independence Day, Potsdam Declaration (1945), *George Bernard Shaw (1856), *US Army Desegregation Day (1944)
27. *Atlantic Telegraph Day, *National Korean War Veterans Armistice Day, *Take Your Houseplant for a Walk Day, *Walk on Stilts Day
28. Peru: Independence Day, Beatrix Potter Day, Thailand: King's Birthday and National Day, World Hepatitis Day, World War I Begins (1914)
29. Global Tiger Day, Lord of the Rings Day, *NASA (1958), Rain Day, Spain: Festival of Near Death Experiences
30. *Emily Brontë (1818), Henry Ford Day, Insulin First Isolated and Extracted Day (1921), National Cheesecake Day, *Paperback Books (1935), United Nations: International Day of Friendship, United Nations: World Day Against Trafficking in Persons, Vanuatu: Independence Day
31. National Mutt Day, *US Patent Office Opened (1790)

Holiday Marketing Ideas

Smart Irrigation Month — Are you aware that smart irrigation is different than just plain irrigation? Well, if you think about it, if you water something in the wrong way, say too much or not enough or with polluted water you could easily kill your plants. Your business is just as fragile. Making the wrong decisions, or even lack of decision, and listening to too much bad advice can dehydrate your business' growth. Therefore, the month of July is the perfect opportunity to host a seminar or webinar that helps others grow their businesses.

Another smart irrigation idea is to help your customers and clients to learn why your products and services are superior to others. Perhaps just a timely eblast with weekly tips about your business offerings would bring a sprout of growth to your income. Touching base with your customers and clients and telling them about your services is a wise thing to do. It is very possible that they may not even know about all the merchandise or services you offer.

Jul 1 Postage Stamp Day — This is one I featured in the 2017 edition of this *Weird & Wacky Holiday Marketing Guide* and is worth repeating.

Imagine all the fun you will have celebrating this Weird & Wacky holiday. Creating postage stamps to share can be quite inspiring, and creative people will probably savor the chance to showcase their designs. So, have a postage stamp design contest.

Another thing you could do is have a Postage Stamp Sized Swap Party! Very simple things, small, delicate, anything that comes close to the size requirements could be fun to swap or trade. Some of the best parties I have attended had prizes that were pretty Weird & Wacky.

If you aren't into either of these ideas, you can always opt for sending out cards with actual stamps on them to your best customers and clients. Better yet, design your own stamp to make your card even more special and uniquely you.

Jul 12 Different Colored Eyes Day—It has been touted that the eyes are the window to the soul. If that's the case, we need to learn to look more closely; not just at eyes but everything around us. Consider taking the time to reevaluate your life, business, clients, customers, and even values. Are you remaining on the course you set for your life and business? If not, make some changes. A Different Colored Eyes Day event is your chance to help others to do likewise. Nevertheless, if because of COVID-19 or you're not feeling up to the challenge and events are not in your marketing toolkit this year, consider going the easy route by sending out a notecard to your best and favorite customers and clients to let them know how unique and special they truly are to you and your business. You see, when you are in contact with them with a card you've taken the time to handwrite and then it turns out that you are mentioning them personally in your correspondence, it will have a larger impact. Enough so, that when they do need your services again, not only will they turn to you, but they just might refer a friend.

Jul 29 Global Tiger Day—Do you have a tiger in your marketing tank? How often do you follow-through with contacting your clients and customers in a timely manner? When you attend a tradeshow where you meet potential new customers do you contact them right away? Procrastination is a very bad habit for a business owner to exhibit.

Perhaps sharing tips on social media or through email today on how to put the tiger back into their marketing or lives would be a wise choice. Start out with some sage advice you may have culled through the years or find a quote or two you can share. Then, to get them to interacting, why not ask them what you could do or offer that would fill a need they might have. Consider their response and if appropriate try to incorporate those changes.

AUGUST

Aug 6 – 15 Sturgis Rally
Aug 24 – Sep 5 Paralympic Games
Aug 30 – Sep 12 US Open Tennis Championship

Month-Long Holidays

American Adventures Month, Black Business Month, Boomers Making a Difference Month, Children's Eye Health and Safety Month, Children's Vision and Learning Month, Happiness Happens Month, International Pirate Month, National Immunization Awareness Month, National Minority Donor Awareness Month, National Spinal Muscular Atrophy Awareness Month, Read-A-Romance Month, What Will Be Your Legacy Month

Week-Long Holidays

Aug 1 – 7 International Clown Week (first full week), National Exercise with Your Child Week, World Breastfeeding Week
Aug 2 – 6 Psychic Week
Aug 8 – 14 Assistance Dog Week
Aug 9 – 13 Perseid Meteor Showers
Aug 11 – 17 Elvis Week
Aug 15 – 21 National Aviation Week
Aug 25 – 31 Be Kind to Humankind Week
Aug 26 – 29 Hotter 'n Hell Hundred Bike Race

Daily Holidays

1. Benin: Independence Day, Emancipation of 500 Day, Fancy Farm Picnic Day, *Girlfriend's Day, *Lughnasadh, Rounds Resounding Day, Sister's Day*, *Spiderman Day, Switzerland: Confederation Day, Trinidad and Tobago: Emancipation Day, United Kingdom: Minden Day, *US Census Day (1790), *US Customs Day, *World Wide Web or Internaut Day (2017)
2. Australia: Picnic Day, Bahamas: Emancipation Day, Canada: Civic Holiday, Colorado Day, Costa Rica: Feast of Our Lady of Angels, *Declaration of Independence: Official Signing (1776), Grenada: Emancipation Day, Iceland and Ireland: August Holiday, Jamaica and Niger: Independence Day, Zambia: Youth Day
3. Columbus Sails for the New World (1492), Equatorial Guinea: Armed Forces Day, Guinea-Bissau: Colonization Martyrs' Day, National Night Out Day, National Watermelon Day, Niger: Independence Day
4. *Louis Armstrong Day, Burkina Faso: Revolution Day, *Coast Guard Day, Queen Elizabeth Day

5. Burkina Faso: Republic Day, Croatia: Homeland Thanksgiving Day, First English Colony in North America (1583)
6. Atomic Bomb Day (1945), Bolivia: Independence Day, Braham Pie Day, Death Penalty Day, *Hiroshima Day, *Jamaica: Independence Achieved (1962), Voting Rights Day (1965)
7. Columbia: Battle of Boyaca Day, Cote D'Ivoire: National Day, Hatfield-McCoy Feud Eruption Day, *Mata Hari Day (1876), National Lighthouse Day, National Mustard Day, *Particularly Preposterous Packaging Day, *Professional Speakers Day, US War Department Day, World Trade Center Tightrope Walk Day
8. *Bonza Bottler Day™, Digital Nomad Day, Happiness Happens Day, Herbert Hoover Day (Sunday nearest Aug 10th), National Fried Chicken and Waffles Day, *Sneak Some Zucchini onto Your Neighbor's Porch Night, Tanzania: Farmers' Day, Wear Your Mother's Jewelry Day
9. Atomic Bomb Day, Islamic New Year, Japan: Moment of Silence (Bombing of Nagasaki), *Moment of Silence Day, Singapore: National Day, South Africa: National Women's Day, *United Nations: International Day of The World's Indigenous People, *Veep Day
10. Bahamas: Fox Hill Day (second Tuesday in August), *Candid Camera Day, Ecuador Independence Day, National S'mores Day, Nestlé Day (1814), *Smithsonian Day, World Lion Day
11. Chadd: Independence Day, *Alex Haley Day (1921), Japan: Yama No Hi (Mountain Day), Saint Clare of Assisi: Feast Day
12. *Home Sewing Machine Day, *IBM PC Day, Night of the Murdered Poets, Thailand: Birthday of the Queen, *United Nations: International Youth Day, *Vinyl Record Day
13. Berlin Wall Erected (1961), Blame Someone Else Day, Central African Republic: Independence Day, Friday the 13th, *Alfred Hitchcock (1899), *International Left Hander's Day, Lucy Stone Day (1818), *Annie Oakley Day (1860), Tunisia: Women's Day
14. China: Double Seven Festival Day, Middle Children's Day, National Garage Sale Day, *Navajo Nation: Code Talkers Day, Pakistan: Independence Day, *Social Security Day, V–J Day (1945)
15. *Assumption of the Virgin Mary, *Best Friends Day, *Chauvin Day, Check the Chip Day, Congo (Brazzaville): National Day, Equatorial Guinea: Constitution Day, Hirohito's Radio Address (1945), India and Korea: Independence Day, Liechtenstein: National Day, *National Relaxation Day, *Panama Canal Day (1914), Transcontinental US Railway Completion (1870), *Woodstock (1969)
16. Canada: Yukon Discovery Day, Dominican Republic: Restoration of the Republic, Klondike Gold Discovery Day, National Roller Coaster Day, Surveillance Day
17. Balloon Crossing of Atlantic Ocean (1978), *Clinton's "Meaning of 'Is' Is" Day (1998), *Davy Crockett (1786), Gabon and Indonesia: Independence Day, *Mae West Day (1893)
18. Ashura: Tenth Day, *Bad Poetry Day, *Birth Control Pills Day, *Mail–Order Catalog Day, National Badge Ribbon Day, Serendipity Day
19. Afghanistan: Independence Day, *Black Cow (Root Beer Float) Day, Don Ho Day (1930), United Nations: World Humanitarian Day
20. Hungary: Saint Stephen's Day, Morocco: Revolution of the King and he People, *Plutonium Day
21. Alexandria Library Sit-in Day, *American Bar Association Day, Hawaii Admission Day Holiday, International Geocaching Day, International Homeless Animals Day˚ and Candlelight Vigils, *Poet's Day, Seminole Tribe Day (1953), United Nations: International Day of Remembrance and Tribute to the Victims of Terrorism
22. *Be an Angel Day, *International Yacht Race Day, Mormon Choir Day, National Bring Your Cat to the Vet Day, *Southern Hemisphere Hoodie-Hoo Day, Vietnam Conflict Begins (1945)

23. First Man-Powered Flight (1977), *United Nations: Day for the Remembrance of the Slave Trade and Its Abolition, *Valentino Day
24. Liberia: Flag Day, *Pluto Demoted Day, Ukraine: Independence Day, *Vesuvius Day, William Wilberforce Day
25. Founders Day, *Kiss-and-Make-Up Day, *National Park Service Day, Uruguay: Independence Day, Spain: La Tomatina (Tomato Food Fight Festival), Uruguay: Independence Day, *Wizard of Oz Day (1939)
26. Baseball Day (First Televised, 1939), Nambia and Philippines: Heroes' Day, *National Dog Day, *Women's Equality Day
27. Moldova: Independence Day, *Mother Teresa Day, *"The Duchess" Who Wasn't Day
28. International Bat Night, *March on Washington (1963), *Race Your Mouse Around the Icons Day, *Radio Commercials Day
29. *According to Hoyle Day, *More Herbs, Less Salt Day, Slovakia: National Uprising Day, United Nations: International Day Against Nuclear Tests
30. Hong Kong: Liberation Day, Family Day in Tennessee, Huey P Long Day, Peru: Saint Rose of Lima Day, Turkey: Victory Day, United Nations: International Day of Victims of Enforced Disappearances
31. Kazakhstan and Kyrgyzstan: Constitution Day and Independence Day, Klondike Eldorado Gold Discovery Day, *Love Litigating Lawyers Day, Malaysia: Freedom Day, Moldova: National Language Day, Trinidad and Tobago: Independence Day

Holiday Marketing Ideas

Black Business Month — Did you know that Black business owners account for about 10 percent of U.S. businesses and about 30 percent of all minority-owned businesses? Furthermore, this year Facebook, the social media giant, has decided to highlight black owned businesses during the entire month of August. And they are partnering with the US Black Chambers for virtual programs Black entrepreneurs can use to help their business as the COVID-19 pandemic rages. Their link is in the Appendix. So, if they are taking advantage of this Weird & Wacky holiday and focusing on virtual events, shouldn't you?

Whether you are an author or a business owner who qualifies for the black business designation this is your month to make a serious marketing push. If you need financial support to make your event a success, why not consider charging a small fee to each business owner to offset your costs. Then, join with other business owners to secure your spot on a "Sidewalk Sale" landing page and spread the word. Their customers may find your offering is much to their liking, which means you will grow your customer base exponentially! When you post on social media be sure to use the hashtag #NationalBlackBusinessMonth.

Aug 1 Girlfriend's Day & Sister's Day — Girlfriends fall into many categories. You may have grown up together or met through work or college. Yet others share a much deeper bond — sisters and mothers. It doesn't surprise me that both of these Weird & Wacky holidays fall on the same day in August. Friendship is one of the most important relationships you will experience and today is your chance to connect with your special friends. Grab a glass of wine and if the pandemic is still in full swing let your friends know how much they mean to you.

This day is about relaxing and reconnecting. You can't work all the time. Take this day off and rekindle those companionships. If you really must do something for your business, use an auto schedule program and set it to send out relationship tips or graphics throughout the day while you are away.

Aug 7 National Lighthouse Day — This holiday calls to me to be a beacon in other people's lives. Why not consider becoming a mentor to a young entrepreneur or child who could use your wisdom and support. I recall when I ran a mentorship program, I actually built my business as I helped others. I never talked about what I did, they just seemed to know and sought my advice and sometimes even hired me for a project they needed designed. Therefore, mentoring someone could be a volunteer effort or it could evolve into a new business relationship. You just never know. If you don't know how to get involved in a mentorship program or how to start one, a good place to start is to refer to my 2013 edition. There you will find "Elements for Effective Practice for Mentoring", courtesy of Mentoring.org along with all the information you need to become a mentor. Be aware that prior to 2014 all *Weird & Wacky Holiday Marketing Guide* publications were only available in digital format.

Additionally, in the 2016 edition you will also find a lighthouse event poster that you can use if you decide to host a National Lighthouse Day Celebration. Just change the name of the event and fill in your event information. This year you'll find a social media graphic in the Appendix that you are free to brand and use.

Aug 10 Nestlé Day — Oh, for the love of chocolate! As we look to celebrate this holiday while seeking a marketing twist, this suggests recipe swaps. Also, consider the characteristics of chocolate, it's lowly beginnings, and the health benefits. All these topics could be great starting points for conversations with your customers and clients.

Chocolate when fist produced is bitter and then with processing becomes the sweet and tasty treat you enjoy. This suggests the *perseverance* and *dedication* that you need to reach your goals. If you are a coach of any kind this is a marvelous marketing direction for you.

Chocolate is produced from the seed of Theobroma cacao seed. It's not even a nut! How's that for a lowly beginning? So, think *seeds of greatness* while you plant them in the minds and hearts of your customers and clients. This can be done with small gestures or an event of gigantic proportions.

Now, for the health benefits, I suggest you look in the Samples Appendix as I have provided a healthy benefit list there. Additionally, it contains more caffeine than coffee, so think energy and alertness or *paying attention*.

Gifts of chocolate to your most loyal customers and clients will wow them — if they aren't allergic. When you take the time to pen a note wishing them a happy Nestlé Day this will go a long way to endearing you to their heart.

Aug 13 International Left Hander's Day — To be born left-handed means growing up in a right-hand world. Learning to adapt is a basic concept that lefties must face every day. So, adapting is your keyword for the day. With COVID-19, businesses all around the globe have had to learn to adapt. Most likely, you have some astute advice you can share on how you adapted that others may not have grasped as of yet.

Sharing tips on how to adapt in the workplace is a great start. There's a wonderful book by Beverly Mahone titled, *The Baby Boomers/Millennial Divide: Making it work at work* that can give you insight on how both sides can adapt to each other.

Daniel Goleman and his co-authors in *The Adaptability Primer* states, "The Adaptability Competency means having flexibility in handling change, being able to juggle multiple demands, and adapting to new situations with fresh ideas or innovative approaches. It means you not only can stay focused on your goals, but also can easily adjust how you achieve them. An adaptable leader can meet new challenges as they arise and not be halted by sudden change, remaining comfortable with the uncertainty that leadership can bring."

I've listed both books in the Resources section so you can easily get your copy. Perhaps after reading them you will come away with some innovative ideas that you too can share.

Aug 26 National Dog Day — To highlight this Weird & Wacky holiday in your marketing plan the first thing that comes to mind is 'loyalty'. Therefore, let the focus be on your most loyal customers and clients. Sharing with them a 'secret' tip or even a discount on a product or service might be an idea worth contemplating.

Another thing they are known for is their role of protector. So, here we have financial, health, personal protection (think aids & skills), and home security. There may be more you can think of, but that will get you thinking in the right direction. These involve tips to share or, if you are up to it, a webinar.

I have crafted a cute social media graphic for you which you'll find in the usual place.

SEPTEMBER

Sep 9 – 18 Canada: Toronto International Film Festival
Sep 15 – Oct 15 National Hispanic Heritage Month
Sep 17 – Oct 3 The Big E
Sep 18 – Oct 3 Oktoberfest

Month-Long Holidays

Atrial Fibrillation Awareness Month, Attention Deficit Hyperactivity Disorder Month, Be Kind to Editors and Writers Month, Childhood Cancer Awareness Month, Chile: National Month, Fall Hat Month, Great American Low-Cholesterol, Low-Fat Pizza Bake, Gynecologic Cancer Awareness Month, Hunger Action Month, Library Card Sign-Up Month, National Cholesterol Education Month, National DNA, Genomics, and Stem Cell Education, and Awareness Month, National Head Lice Prevention Month, National Honey Month, National Mushroom Month, *National Preparedness Month, National Prostate Cancer Awareness Month, National Recovery Month, National Rice Month, National Service Dog Month, One-On-One Month, Ovarian Cancer Awareness Month, Pleasure Your Mate Month, September Is Healthy Aging® Month, Shameless Promotion Month, Sports Eye Safety Month, Subliminal Communications Month, Update Your Résumé Month, Whole Grains Month, Worldwide Speak Out Month, Youth Leadership Month

Week-Long Holidays

Sep 1 – 7 Brazil: Independence Week
Sep 3 – 4 Wisconsin State Coe-Chip Throw
Sep 3 – 10 Substitute Teacher Appreciation Week
Sep 6 – 10 National Payroll Week
Sep 7 – 11 Play Days
Sep 12 – 18 United Kingdom: Battle of Britain Week
Sep 13 – 18 National Line Dance Week
Sep 13 – 19 Be a Mensch Week
Sep 17 – 23 Constitution Week
Sep 19 – 25 Build a Better Image Week, International Go-Kart Week, International Week of the Deaf, National Farm Safety and Health Week, National Security Officer Appreciation Week, Tolkien Week, World Reflexology Week
Sep 20 – 26 International Women's Ecommerce Days
Sep 21 – 27 Sukkot, Succoth, or Feast of the Tabernacles
Sep 26 – Oct 2 Banned Books Week — Celebrating the Freedom to Read

Daily Holidays

1. Chicken Boy's Birthday, *Edgar Rice Burroughs (1875) *Emma M. Nutt Day, Japan: Kanto Earthquake Memorial Day, National Toy Testing Day, Orthodox Ecclesiastical New Year, Slovakia: Constitution Day, Titanic Discovery Day, Uzbekistan: Independence Day, WWII Begins (1939)
2. Benton Neighbor Day, Calendar Adjustment Day, US Treasury Department Founded Day, Vietnam: Independence Day, *V–J Day
3. Bring Your Manners to Work Day, Penny Press Day (1833), Qatar: Independence Day, San Marino: National Day
4. Curaçao: Animal's Day, Electric Lights Day, *Newspaper Carrier Day, *Paul Harvey Day
5. First Continental Congress Assembly (1774), First Labor Day Observance (1882), Jesse James Day (1847), Michigan's Great Fire of 1881, United Nations: International Day of Charity
6. Jane Addams Day, Baltic States: Independence Day, Bulgaria: Unification Day, Canada and US: Labor Day (first Monday in September), Pakistan: Defense of Pakistan Day, Rosh Hashanah (begins at sundown), Swaziland: Independence Day, United Nations: Millennium Summit (1955)
7. Brazil: Independence Day, *Google Commemoration Day (1998), *Grandma Moses Day, Mouthguard Day, *Neither Snow nor Rain Day–Day, Queen Elizabeth I Birthday (1533), Rosh Hashanah or Jewish New Year
8. Andorra: National Holiday, Huey P. Long Shot Day, Macedonia: Independence Day, Malta: Victory Day, Pediatric Hematology/Oncology Nurses Day, Star Trek Day, Tarzan Day, *United Nations: International Literacy Day
9. *Bonza Bottler Day™, Japan: Chrysanthemum Day, Korea, Democratic People's Republic of: National Day, Luxembourgh: Liberation Ceremony, Tajikistan: Independence Day, *Wonderful Weirdos Day
10. Belize: Saint George's Caye Day, China: Teacher's Day, National Day of Prayer and Remembrance, National Dog Walker Appreciation Day, Swap Ideas Day, World Suicide Prevention Day
11. *Attack on America Day, Catalonia: National Day of Catalonia, Ethiopia: New Year's Day, *Food Stamps Day, *Patriot Day and National Day of Service and Remembrance, Prairie Day
12. Defenders Day, Guinea-Bissau: National Holiday, National Grandparents' Day, United Nations: Day for South-South Cooperation, Video Games Day
13. 9 x 13 Day, Kids Take Over the Kitchen Day, *National Celiac Awareness Day, Roald Dahl Day, Scooby Doo Day
14. Gravitational Waves First Detected (2015), Nicaragua: Battle of San Jacinto Day, *Solo Transatlantic Balloon Crossing (1984), United Nations: Opening Day of General Assembly
15. *Agatha Christie Day, Costa Rica and El Salvador: Independence Day, *First National Convention for Blacks (1830), Guatemala and Honduras: Independence Day, National School Backpack Awareness Day, Nicaragua: Independence Day, Quarterly Estimated Federal Income Tax Payers' Due Date (also Jan 15, Apr 15, and June 15, 2021), United Kingdom: Battle of Britain Day, *United Nations: International Day of Democracy
16. *Anne Bradstreet Day, Cherokee Strip Day, General Motors Day, *Great Seal of the US (1782), Malaysia: Malaysia Day (Hari Malaysia), Mayflower Day (1620), Mexico: Independence Day, Papua New Guinea: Independence Day, *United Nations: International Day for the Preservation of the Ozone Layer, World Play-Doh Day
17. Angola: Day of the National Hero, *Citizenship Day, *Constitution Day (1787), National Constitution Center Constitution Day, National Football League Formed Day (1920), National

POW/MIA Recognition (the third Friday in September), National Table Shuffleboard Day, VFW Ladies Auxiliary Day
18. Chili: Independence Day, International Coastal Cleanup, International Red Panda Day, Locate and Old Friend Day, National Cheeseburger Day, National HIV/AIDS and Aging Awareness Day, *US Air Force Birthday, *US Capitol Cornerstone Laid, US Takes Out its First Loan (1789)
19. *"Iceman" Mummy Discovered (1991), *International Talk Like a Pirate Day, Saint Christopher (Saint Kitts) and Nevis: Independence Day
20. 20. *Billie Jean King Wins Battle of the Sexes (1973), Financial Panic Day, Fonzie Jumps the Shark Day, International Day of University Sport, Japan: Respect for the Aged Day, *National Equal Rights Founded (1884), Sukkot (begins at sundown)
21. Armenia, Belize, and Malta: Independence Day, IT Professionals Day, Korea: Chuseok, National Surgical Technologists Day, *United Nations: International Day of Peace
22. American Business Woman's Day, Dear Diary Day, *Emancipation Proclamation (1862), Hobbit Day, Ice Cream Cone Day, International Day of Radiant Peace, Japan: Autumnal Equinox Day, Long Count Day (1927), Mabon (Alban Elfed), Mali: Independence Day, National Centenarian's Day, National Walk 'n' Roll Dog Day, Remote Employee Appreciation Day, US Postmaster General's Day (1789)
23. Baseball's Greatest Dispute Day, *Celebrate Bisexuality Day, Checkers Day, Innergize Day, *Lewis and Clark Expedition Returns (1806), Planet Neptune Discovery (1846), Remember Me Thursday®, Saudi Arabia: Kingdom Unification, United Nations: International Day of Sign Languages
24. Cambodia: Constitutional Declaration Day, Daniel Boone Day, Guinea-Bissau: Independence Day, Hug a Vegan Day, Mozambique: Armed Forces Day, *National Punctuation Day, Schwenkfelder Thanksgiving, South Africa: Heritage Day
25. *First American Newspaper Published (1690), *Greenwich Mean Time Begins (1676), National Hunting and Fishing Day, National One Hit Wonder Day, National Psychotherapy Day, National Public Lands Day, Pacific Ocean Discovered (1513) Rwanda: Republic Day
26. *Johnny Appleseed Day, Gold Star Mother's and Family Day (always the last Sunday in September), International Day of the Deaf, United Nations: International Day for the Total Elimination of Nuclear Weapons
27. *Samuel Adams (1722), *Ancestor Appreciation Day, Ethiopia: True Cross Day, Saint Vincent de Paul Feast Day, *World Tourism Day
28. *Cabrillo Day, Taiwan: Confucius and Teachers' Day, United Nations/UNESCO: International Day for Universal Access to Information, World Rabies Day
29. Michelangelo Antonio (1912), Michaelmas, *National Attend Your Grandchild's Birth Day, National Biscotti Day, National Coffee Day, Paraguay: Boquerón Day, Scotland Yard Day (1829), Simchat Torah, Veterans of Foreign Wars Day
30. Botswana: Independence Day, First Criminal Execution in America Day (1630), Gutenberg Bible Published (1452), International Translation Day, Saint Jerome: Feast Day, United Nations: World Maritime Day

Holiday Marketing Ideas

Worldwide Speak Out Month — This Weird & Wacky holiday is set forth to hone your speaking skills with both small intimate group settings and public speaking arenas. Therefore, it should be obvious what your focus should be this month. If you are a Toastmasters member, you probably have a good handle on this. However, for those of you that fear speaking out even in small group settings, it is time to get the help you need. Even you can schedule a mini-conference, webinar, or Facebook live event and bring in experts who can share their tips and tricks throughout the month.

Besides events, consider compiling some tips to share either on social media or emails. This does mean you will have to search books and websites that you can glean wisdom from. To that end, the first book I ever wrote was on public speaking and has been reviewed to high acclaim by none other than the author of For Dummy's PowerPoint book. Take a look. The link is in the Appendix. I know, shameless plug, but …

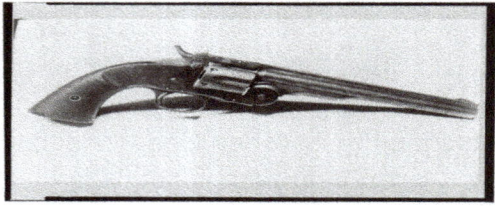

Sep 5 Jesse James Day — Today we focus on the day that Jesse James met his match in Northfield, Minnesota. Triumphing over the things that stand in your way of success should be your focus today. Some of the fears you can help others overcome include the fear of speaking in public, since it is indeed Worldwide Speak Out Month that's a good start; fear of failure; fear of success, yup that's a real fear; fear of the telephone; fear of proximity to others. I am sure you can think of a few more, but that should get you started. As you can see these fears could be debilitating to a business owner, so helping them learn how to overcome them is something they will thank you for. Remember, it is a series of small steps that get you to your goal.

With your topic chosen, your task is at hand. Share some tips or tweets throughout the day that will help others become victorious.

Sep 11 Food Stamps Day — It's time to organize a food drive. In the Sample Appendix you will find everything you need to organize your food drive including a Sample Food Drive List, Tips on Generating Publicity, and a Food Drive Flyer by AARP. Surround yourself with those who will support your food drive, you can't do it all by yourself. If you want to do it right, let the media know what you are doing. Once the word gets out you may find yourself being interviewed on talk radio or news shows.

Sep 18 International Red Panda Day — Red pandas live in the Himalayas and China. They are also called firefox. The word 'firefox' reminds me of the internet which in turn brings to mind how important the internet is to humans on planet earth. Things to do today, besides bringing awareness to their diminishing numbers while fundraising in partnership with your local zoo, is to consider how much you actually do on the internet. Most of your day is probably tied to it in one way or another. As you ponder this, consider tweets and posts that reflect your daily interactions that employ this means of communication.

If you want to stick closer to the subject, you could simply post facts about these interesting mammals. In the Resources section you will find a link to a YouTube video that shares a lot of facts you can cull from.

Sep 22 Remote Employee Appreciation Day — So many businesses have gone remote in 2020 due to the pandemic that celebrating them on their special day seems like the appropriate response in 2021.

To that end, there are numerous things you could do to make their day extra special. If you can afford to, give them a gift certificate for a coffee or online shop, or even a diner in their area. If your budget is a bit more limited a card is always appropriate. Be sure to hand write it and send it so it will arrive prior to today. Don't just say thanks or wish them a happy REA day. Make it personal by mentioning something they particularly did that impressed you.

OCTOBER

Oct 7 Rabi'i: The Month of Migration (begins)
Oct 24 – Nov 11 World Origami Days

Month-Long Holidays

Adopt-A-Shelter-Dog Month, Antidepressant Death Awareness Month, Breast Cancer Awareness Month, Celebrating the Bilingual Child Month, Contact Lens Safety Month, Domestic Violence Awareness Month, Dyslexia Awareness Month, Gay and Lesbian History Month, German American Heritage Month, Global Diversity Awareness Month, Go Hog Wild — Eat Country Ham Month, Health Literacy Month, Inktober, National Audiology Awareness Month, *National Breast Cancer Awareness Month, National Bullying Prevention Awareness Month, National Chiropractic Health Month, National Crime Prevention Month, *National Cybersecurity Awareness Month, National Dental Hygiene Month, National Depression Education and Awareness Month, *National Disability Employment Awareness Month, *National Domestic Violence Awareness Month, National Down Syndrome Awareness Month, National Liver Awareness Month, National Medical Librarians Month, National Orthodontic Health Month, National Physical Therapy Month, National Polish American Heritage Month, National Popcorn Poppin' Month, National Reading Group Month, National Roller Skating Month, National Seafood Month, National Spina Bifida Awareness Month, National Stamp Collecting Month, National Stop Bullying Month, National Work and Family Month, Organize Your Medical Information Month, Positive Attitude Month, Rett Syndrome Awareness Month, Squirrel Awareness and Appreciation Month, Vegetarian Awareness Month, Workplace Politics Awareness Month, World Menopause Month

Week-Long Holidays

Oct 3 – 9 Fire Prevention Week, Getting the World to Beat a Path to Your Door Week, Mental Illness Awareness Week, National Carry a Tune Week
Oct 4 – 8 Industrial Water Week, National Work from Home Week
Oct 4 – 10 United Nations: World Space Week
Oct 8 – 10 Apple Butter Makin' Days
Oct 8 – 16 Canada: Kitchener-Waterloo Oktoberfest
Oct 9 – 10 Chowder Days
Oct 10 – 16 Earth Science Week, Emergency Nurses Week, National Food Bank Week, National Metric Week
Oct 10 – 17 Take Your Medicine Americans Week
Oct 11 – 15 National School Lunch Week
Oct 15 – 20 Japan: Newspaper Week

Oct 17 – 23 Bullying Bystanders Unite Week, Food and Drug Interaction Education and Awareness Week National Character Counts Week, National Chemistry Week, National Forest Products Week, Rodent Awareness Week

Oct 18 – 22 Nuclear Science Week

Oct 18 – 24 Careers in Energy Week

Oct 20 – 24 Germany: Frankfurt Book Fair

Oct 24 – 30 United Nations: Disarmament Week

Oct 24 – 31 Prescription Errors Education and Awareness Week

Oct 25 – 31 International Magic Week

Daily Holidays

1. Cyberspace Day, Cyprus: Independence Day, Disney World Day, *Fire Pup Day, Kids Music Day, Model-T Day, National Diversity Day, Nigeria: Independence Day, Night of the Living Dead Day, South Korea: Armed Forces Day, This is Your Life Day, Tuvalu: Independence Day, United Nations: International Day of Older Persons, US 2021 Federal Fiscal Year Begins, World Smile Day, World Vegetarian Day
2. Bed and Breakfast Inn Mascot Day, Gandhi Day, *Guardian Angels Day, Guinea: Independence Day, *Groucho Marx (1890), *National Custodial Workers Day, *"Peanuts" Debut Day (1950), 'Twilight Zone' Day, United Nations: International Day of Nonviolence, World Day for Farmed Animals
3. Blessing of the Fishing Fleet, Captain Kangaroo Day, Country Inn, Bed-and-Breakfast Day, Germany: Day of German Unity, Honduras: Francisco Morazán Holiday, Korea: Tangun Day (National Foundation Day), *Mickey Mouse Club Day (1955), National G.E.O. (Growth. Overcome.Empower) Day, Netherlands: Relief of Leiden Day, World Communion Sunday
4. Child Health Day (first Monday in October), *Dick Tracy Day (1931), *Greorgian Calendar Adjustment Day, International Ships-In-Bottles Day, Lesotho: Independence Day, National Taco Day, *Ten-Four Day, United Nations: World Habitat Day, World Child Development Day, World Day of Bullying Prevention™
5. Duputren Disease Awareness Day, James Bond Day, Portugal: Republic Day, *United Nations: World Teachers Day
6. *American Library Association Day, Egypt: Armed Forces Day, International Walk to School Day, Ireland: Ivy Day, *Jackie Mayer Rehab Day, *National German-American Day, National Noodle Day, Random Acts of Poetry Day, United Kingdom: National Badger Day
7. National Depression Screening Day, United Kingdom: national Poetry Day
8. *Alvin C. York Day, Croatia: Statehood Day, *Great Chicago Fire (1871), National Hydrogen and Fuel Cell Day, National Pierogy Day, National Salmon Day, Peshtigo Forest Fire (1871)
9. 9. International Migratory Bird Day, Korea: Hangul (Alphabet Day), *Leif Erickson Day, National Nanotechnology Day, Peru: Day of National Honor, Uganda: Independence Day, *United Nations: World Post Day, Universal Music Day
10. *Bonza Bottler Day™, *Double 10 Day, Grandmother's Day in Florida, National Handbag Day, Samoa and American Samoa: White Sunday, *Tuxedo Day, *US Naval Academy Day, World Day Against the Death Penalty, *World Mental Health Day
11. *Adding Machine Day, Canada: Thanksgiving Day, Columbus Day, Discoverer's Day in Hawaii, Fiji: Independence Day, *General Pulaski Memorial Day, Indigenous Peoples" Day, Japan: Sports Day, *National Coming Out Day, National Kick Butt Day, Native Americans' Day (South

Dakota), Southern Food Heritage Day, United Nations: International Day of the Girl Child, Yorktown Victory Day

12. Ada Lovelace Day, Bahamas Discovery Day, Columbus Day (Traditional), *Day of the Six–Billion, Equatorial Guinea: Independence Day, International Face Your Fears Day, *International Moment of Frustration Scream Day, Mexico: Dia de la Raza, Spain: National Holiday
13. *Jesse Leroy Brown Day, Emergency Nurses Day, Israel: Aliyah Day (Yom Ha'Aliyah), National Bring Your Teddy Bear to Work Day, National Bullying Prevention Day, National Fossil Day, National Take Your Parents to Lunch Day, *Navy Birthday, United Nations: International Day for Natural Disaster Reduction, Whitehouse Cornerstone Laid (1792)
14. *Be Bald and Be Free Day, Sound Barrier Broken (1947), Supersonic Skydive Day (2012)
15. *Blind Americans Equality Day (formerly White Cane Safety Day), First Manned Flight (1783), Get to Know Your Customers Day (third Thursday of each quarter is set aside to get to know your customers even better), India: Dasara(Dussehra), *National Boss' Day (Observed), National Grouch Day, National Mammography Day, United Nations: International Day of Rural Women
16. Birth Control Day (1916), Dictionary Day, Global Cat Day, Million Man March (1995), Sweetest Day, United Nations: World Food Day, Noah Webster Day
17. Black Poetry Day, Evel Knievel Day, Monster Myths by Moonlight, *Mulligan Day, National Playing Card Collection Day, San Francisco 1989 Earthquake (1989), *United Nations: International Day for the Eradication of Poverty
18. Azerbaijan: Independence Day, Canada: Persons Day (1929), Comic Strip Day, Jamaica: National Heroes Day, Saint Luke Feast Day, Virgin Islands: Hurricane Thanksgiving Day, Water Pollution Control Day, *World Menopause Day
19. Alaska Day, Evaluate Your Life Day, LGBT Center Awareness Day, Yorktown Day
20. John Dewey Day, Guatemala: Revolution Day, Hagfish Day, Kenya: Mashujaa Day, Miss America Rose Day, Missouri Day
21. Get Smart About Credit Day, Get to Know Your Customers Day (third Thursday of each quarter is set aside to get to know your customers even better), *Incandescent Lamp Day, Taiwan: Overseas Chinese Day
22. *International Stuttering Awareness Day, Smart is Cool Day, World's End Day
23. Cambodia: Peace Treaty Day, Hungary: Republic Day (Declares Independence), *IPod Day, National Mole Day, Swallows Depart from San Juan Capistrano, Thailand: Chulalongkorn Day
24. First Barrel Jump over Niagara Falls (1901), Mother-In-Law Day, Recycle Your Mercury Thermostat Day, United Nations Day, *United Nations: World Development Information Day
25. First Female FBI Agents (1972), New Zealand: Labor Day, Picasso Day, Saint Crispin's Day, Sourest Day, Taiwan: Retrocession Day, Zambia: Independence Day
26. Austria: National Day, Erie Canal Day, Gunfight at the O.K. Corral (1881), Mule Day
27. *Cranky Coworkers Day, *Navy Day, Saint Vincent and the Grenadines, and Turkmenistan: Independence Day, United Nations: World Day for Audiovisual Heritage, *Walt Disney Day
28. Czech Republic: Independence Day, Greece: Ochi Day, *Saint Jude's Day, Statue of Liberty Dedication (1886)
29. Frankenstein Friday, *Internet Created (1969), National Cat Day, Turkey: Republic Day
30. Checklists Day, *Create A Great Funeral Day, Devil's Night, *Haunted Refrigerator Night, National Candy Corn Day, *Emily Post Day, "War of the Worlds" (1938), World Audio Drama Day
31. *Books for Treats Day, "Car Talk" Day, European Union: Daylight Savings Time Ends, *Halloween or All Hallows' Eve, Houdini Day, *Magic Day, Mount Rushmore Day, *National

Knock–Knock Day, *Reformation Sunday, Samhain, Taiwan: Chiang Kai-Shek Day, Trick or Treat or Beggar's Night, United Nations: World Cities Day

Holiday Marketing Ideas

Squirrel Awareness and Appreciation Month — Squirrels are a creature in perpetual motion. They scurry from hither to yon with a mission and purpose. They plan for the future and can be found in every clime in the world. As you probably personally observed, they are both smart and cleaver. So, to utilize Squirrel Awareness and Appreciation Month in your marketing efforts, business building and career and financial planning are topics you may want to embrace. How about time management practices? A theme you might use is, "Don't squirrel away your time." Whether you choose to hold weekly webinars, or share tips and tweets throughout the month, the results will be reflected in the amount of planning and preparation you do.

Oct 1 World Smile Day — How many smiles can you give away today? The funny thing about smiles is that they come in many styles. The way you smile can say more than the smile itself. They can be quirky, coy, sly, a toothy grin, a smirk, pasted on, polite, a caught or oops smile, and numerous others. In all their vagueness and assortment, smiles are one of the most potent means we have of communicating who we are and what we intend.

Did you ever consider that a smile is not a smile if you don't leave it behind? Whether that means giving it away or leaving remnants of it lingering on your countenance, a sincere smile must touch something or someone to be truly effective. Therefore, share your smile and words of encouragement with everyone you touch today. If you are looking for a graphic you can share on social media, you'll find it in the Samples Appendix.

Oct 10 National Handbag Day — Today we celebrate the lowly tote most women and some men carry with them each and every day. They are not only a vital accessory but they're also a fashion statement that comes in all shapes, colors, and sizes. To make today a fun marketing day host a photo contest for the most unique, weirdest, ugliest, beautiful, etc., purses you and your clients and friends possess. The only rule is they have to own it. It can't be just a photo they found on the internet.

If you want to make it even more fun, host a party! Add to that photo contest a game or two, like they get a prize if they have … in their purse. I saw this done years ago on Let's Make a Deal, I think. Or how about show me "#" things that begin with the letter "?". Now it's your turn to think of some appropriate games.

For those of you who enjoy the ease of posting social media graphics, you will find one I have created for you to use in the Samples Appendix.

Oct 15 National Grouch Day — Irritable. Cranky. Pessimistic. Miserable. These are the characteristics of a grouch. While grouches can be thorny, they are still lovable (Sesame Street's Oscar) and therefore deserving of the time in the spotlight. So, while you make way for Oscar and his friends, let them know you're thinking about them by posting your Happy National Grouch Day wishes on all your social media channels. Then there's always the movies about grouches you could end your day with such as Grouchy Old Men, The Grinch, or my favorite, Second Hand Lion.

To gear it toward an event, you might even help others discover how to deal with the grouches in their lives. Sometimes that means even firing a client or customer. But be aware that a grouch is not a bully, so don't get them confused.

Oct 29 National Cat Day—Just prior to Halloween the cat takes the forefront. This is quite timely since in just a few days the cat plays a less significant role to the witches, ghosts, and goblins that will be lurking in your neighborhood. So, to use National Cat Day as a marketing event there are many things you could possibly do, one of which is volunteer at your local SPCA. If you aren't the volunteer type you could always promote an adopt a cat program in your area. I would think the SPCA would be grateful for your help in this area as well and could give you some advice on organizing your drive. If you can convince a pet supply stores or even bookstores to help sponsor your efforts, you might even attract some media attention. And we all know what a bit of media attention can do for your business.

NOVEMBER

Nov 18 – Dec 30 Germany: Duisburg Christmas Market
Nov 28 – Jan 6, 2022 Netherlands: Midwinter Horn Blowing
Nov 22 – Dec 22 Germany: Frankfurt Christmas Market

Month-Long Holidays

American Diabetes Month, Aviation History Month, Banana Pudding Lovers Month, Diabetic Eye Disease Month, Eye Donation Month, Hepatitis C (HCV) Education, Awareness, and Screening Month, Lung Cancer Awareness Month, Movember, *National Adoption Month, National Epilepsy Awareness Month, *National Family Caregivers Month, National Georgia Pecan Month, National Inspirational Role Models Month, National Long-Term Care Awareness Month, National Marrow Awareness Month, National Memoir Writing Month, *National Native American Heritage Month, National Novel Writing Month, National Runaway Prevention Month, Peanut Butter Lovers' Month, Picture Book Month, World Vegan Month, Worldwide Bereaved Siblings Awareness Month

Week-Long Holidays

Nov 1 – 5 National Patient Accessibility Week
Nov 7 – 13 Polar Bear Week
Nov 8 – 12 National Young Reader's Week
Nov 12 – 14 National Donor Sabbath
Nov 13 – 19 World Antibiotic Awareness Week (tentative)
Nov 15 – 19 American Education Week
Nov 21 – 27 National Family Week

Daily Holidays

1. Algeria: Revolution Day, *All Hallows or All Saints Day, Antigua and Barbuda: Independence Day, Australia: Recreation Day, European Union (1993), European Union Day, Extra Mile Day, Lisbon Earthquake (1755), Mexico: Day of the Dead, *National Authors' Day, National Forgiveness and Happiness Day, National Sports Fan Day, US Virgin Islands: Liberty Day
2. *All Souls Day, Daniel Boone Day, *First Scheduled Radio Broadcast (1920), General Election Day, National Broadcast Traffic Professionals Day, United Nations: International Day to End Impunity for Crimes Against Journalists
3. Canada: New Inuit Territory Approved (1992), *Cliché Day, Dewey Day, Dominica: National Day, *Japan: Culture Day, Micronesia and Panama: Independence Day, Public Television Day, *Sandwich Day, SOS Day

4. Israel: Sigid, India: Diwali (Deepavali), Italy: Victory Day, *King Tut Tomb Discovery (1922), Mischief Night, National Easy Bake Oven Day, National Men Make Dinner Day, Panama: Flag Day, Return Day, Russia: Unity Day, UNESCO Day, *Will Rogers (1879)
5. El Salvador: Day of the First Shout for Independence, *England: Guy Fawkes Day, Fountain Pen Day, Vivian Leigh–Scarlett O'Hara Day (1913), *Shattered Backboard Day, National Medical Science Liaison (MSL) Awareness and Appreciation Day, Samoa: Arbor Day, United Nations: World Tsunami Awareness Day
6. Birth of Bab, Morocco: Anniversary of the Green March, National Bison Day, Pumpkin Destruction Day, Sadie Hawkins Day, Saxophone Day, Sweden: All Saints' Day and Gustavus Adolphus Day, *United Nations: International Day for Preventing the Exploitation of the Environment in War and Armed Conflict
7. Bangladesh: Solidarity Day, Madam Curie Day, Daylight Savings Time Ends: Standard Time Resumes, First Black Governor Elected (1989), Republican Symbol (1874), Russia: Revolution Day, Zero Tasking Day
8. Abet and Aid Punsters Day, Cook Something Bold and Pungent Day, Fill Our Staplers Day, Shakespeare Authorship Mystery Day, *X-ray Day
9. *Berlin Wall Opened (1989), Boston Fire (1872), Cambodia: Independence Day, East Coast Blackout (1965), Germany: Kristallnacht, National Child Safety Council Day, Vietnam Veterans Memorial Statue Unveiling (1984)
10. *Area Code Day (1951), Marine Corps Day, Panama: First Shout of Independence, Claude Rains Day, Sesame Street Anniversary (1969), United Nations: World Science Day for Peace and Development
11. Angola: Independence Day, *Bonza Bottler Day™, Canada: Remembrance Day, China: Singles Day, Columbia: Cartagena Independence Day, Death/Duty Day, England: Remembrance Day, God Bless America Day, Japan: Origami Day, Maldives: Republic Day, Poland: Independence Day, Sweden: Saint Martin's Day, Switzerland: Martinmas Goose (Martinigians), Veterans Day (1919)
12. Mexico: Postman's Day, World Pneumonia Day
13. Holland Tunnel Day
14. Dow Jones Tops 1,000 (1642), Germany: Volkstrauertag, Guinea-Bissau: Readjustment Movement's Day, India: Children's Day, Loosen Up Lighten Up Day, Moby Dick Day, Claude Monet Day, National Block It Out Day, *United Nations: World Diabetes Day
15. *America Recycles Day, Belgium: Dynasty Day, Brazil: Republic Day, George Spelvin Day, Japan: Shichi-Go-San (Seven-Five-Three) Day, National Bundt Day
16. Estonia: Day of National Rebirth, *Lewis and Clark Expedition Reaches Pacific Ocean (1805), Saint Eustatius, *United Nations: International Day for Tolerance
17. Germany: Buss Und Bettag, *Homemade Bread Day, National Book Awards Announcement Day, National Educational Support Professionals Day, National Unfriend Day, Suez Canal Day, World Prematurity Day
18. Great American Smoke-out (third Thursday), Haiti: Army Day, Latvia: Independence Day, Married to a Scorpio Support Day, Mickey Mouse Day, Oman: National Holiday, US Uniform Time Zone Plan Day, World Philosophy Day
19. Belize: Garifuna Day, Cold War Ends (1990), *Dedication Day (1862), First Automatic Toll Collection Machine (1954), Gandhi Day, Garfield Day, *"Have A Bad Day" Day, Monaco: National Holiday, Puerto Rico: Discovery Day, Substitute Educators Day, United Nations: World Toilet Day

20. *Bill of Rights Day, Edwin Powell Hubble Day, *Mandelbrot Day (1924), Mexico: Revolution Day, *Name Your PC Day, Transgender Day of Remembrance, *United Nations: African Industrialization Day, United Nations: Universal Children's Day
21. *Sir Samuel Cunard (1787), Dow Jones Tops 5,000, Germany: Totensonntag, Stir It Up Sunday, United Nations: World Day of Remembrance for Road Traffic Victims, *United Nations: World Television Day, World Hello Day
22. Charles De Gaulle Day 1890), *George Eliot (1819), Lebanon: Independence Day, Switzerland: Zibelemarit (Onion Market), Edward Teach "Blackbeard" Death, (1718)
23. Billy the Kid Day, Fibonacci Day, Japan: Labor Thanksgiving Day, Boris Karloff Day, Harpo Marx Day
24. *Dale Carnegie (1888), *Celebrate Your Unique Talent Day, *D.B. Cooper Day, Tie One On Day™
25. Bosnia and Herzegovina: National Day, *Andrew Carnegie (1835), *JFK Day (1960), Saint Catherine's Day, Suriname: Independence Day, Thanksgiving Day United Nations: International Day for the Elimination of Violence Against Women Day
26. Black Friday, Buy Nothing Day (27–28), Dine Over Your Kitchen Sink Day, Family Day in Nevada, Mongolia: Republic Day, National Flossing Day, Native American Heritage Day, Charles Schultz (1922), World Olive Tree Day
27. Face Transplant Day, International Aura Awareness Day, Laerdal Tunnel Opening (2000), Bruce Lee Day, Slinky™ Day, Small Business Saturday
28. Advent First Sunday, *Albania: Independence Day, Chad: Republic Day, Chanukah (begins at sundown), Handel's Messiah Sing-Along Day, *Lévi–Strauss (1908), Mauritania: Independence Day, Panama: Independence from Spain
29. Alcott Day, Chanukah, Cider Monday, Cyber Monday, *Electronic Greetings Day, *CS Lewis (1898), *United Nations: International Day of Solidarity with the Palestinian People
30. Articles of Peace Between Great Britain and the US (1782), Barbados: Independence Day, Computer Security Day, Giving Tuesday, Philippines: Bonifacio Day, Saint Andrew's Day, *Stay Home Because You're Well Day, United Nations: Day of Remembrance for all Victims of Chemical Warfare

Holiday Marketing Ideas

National Adoption Month — This month's focus being adoption consider focusing on adopting good habits to replace bad ones. As you help others answer this call, you'll find that events are always a good idea. Since it is a month-long holiday, you will have the benefit from choosing how long or short your event will be. Everything from time management to relaxation are topics on which you could emphasize.

Nov 1 National Authors' Day — Author and avid reader fans, this is your day to cheer. Offering a reading list to your customers and clients that will help them grow in a positive direction — if you are neither — would be a viable alternative. For those of us who are of the former persuasion, look toward doing book readings, character interviews, blog tours, or offering a discount coupon. These could all work for you.

Nov 6 Saxophone Day — The memories of the sultry tones of a sax bring to mind sax legends like Coleman Hawkins, Lester Young, Stan Getz, Sonny Rollins, John Coltrane, and Kenny G. As you spend the day today why not pull up some of your

favorite jazz sax artists and enjoy your artists of choice? While you are at it, consider sharing your love by posting facts about some of them on your social media spaces? Start a discussion with your contacts and you might just discover a new favorite. Oh, and by the way, did you know that there are four different types of sax's? They are baritone, tenor, alto, and soprano. The soprano sax lacks the curve of the others. Those are facts you could share that are probably not well known. Look in the Samples Appendix for a graphic you can brand and use if you want something easy to do.

Another idea is to focus on the mood that a good sax melody can create. Candles and bath products, maybe even a good glass of wine are all tools that can enhance your experience. So, those of you who proffer those items as well as stress relief coaches would do well to set the mood at a live or online event. Perhaps going as far as offering a popular sax CD to all those in attendance who purchase over a certain dollar amount of products is something you should contemplate. This is something that the PBS fundraising drive team uses every year. Why shouldn't you take their lead and do the same?

Nov 14 National Block It Out Day — Today is about stamping out cyberbullying. Bullying touches the lives of our children and youth both online and off — and affects adults both in their cars and workplaces. No one is entirely immune to its devastating effects. Therefore, today it is imperative we educate ourselves and our children how unacceptable even the smallest slight posted or given could lead to dire consequences both for the recipient and the bully.

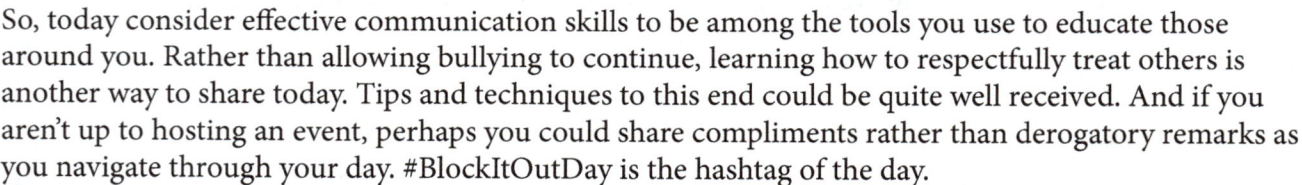

As you shed light on this mal-intent, sharing how to block out the cyberbullies is just the beginning. Ross Ellis, the CEO and Founder of STOMP Out Bullying™ states, "STOMP Out Bullying is the nation's leading anti-bullying organization, whose efforts seek to reduce and prevent online bullying in all of its forms. With the goal to eliminate digital abuse, they educate youth about homophobia, LGBT discrimination, hatred and racism, and promote online civility and inclusion."

So, today consider effective communication skills to be among the tools you use to educate those around you. Rather than allowing bullying to continue, learning how to respectfully treat others is another way to share today. Tips and techniques to this end could be quite well received. And if you aren't up to hosting an event, perhaps you could share compliments rather than derogatory remarks as you navigate through your day. #BlockItOutDay is the hashtag of the day.

Nov 27 International Aura Awareness Day — It is strongly believed that our aura has a strong impact on our health and wellbeing. There are those that can read auras and by doing so provide insight into a person's beliefs, thoughts, and personalities. The possible colors range from red to white each with a different meaning. To celebrate this day, you could host an event in which among other things you could allow your attendees to have their aura read. It may be easier to connect with an aura reader or spiritual healer who is holding an event on this day. You might learn how to read auras yourself or how your physical body connects to your spiritual and emotional body and ties in to your overall health. At the very least share your well wishes on your social media channels and if you are looking for the hashtag, it is #InternationalAuraAwarenessDay.

DECEMBER

Dec 1 – Jan 6 Netherlands: Midwinter Horn Blowing
Dec 14 – Jan 5, 2022 Christmas Bird Count
Dec 14 – 28 Halcyon Days
Dec 15 – Jan 6, 2022 Puerto Rico: Navidades

Month-Long Holidays

Bingo's Birthday Month, Give the Gift of Sight Month, Honor Your Pharmacists Month, *National Impaired Driving Prevention Month, National Write a Business Plan Month, Safe Toys and Gifts Month, Worldwide Food Service Safety Month

Week-Long Holidays

Dec 3 – 10 Clerc-Gallaudet Week
Dec 6 – 10 Older Driver Safety Awareness Week
Dec 10 – 17 Human Rights Week
Dec 17 – 23 Saturnalia
Dec 16 – 24 Mexico: Posadas
Dec 26 – Jan 1, 2022 Kwanzaa

Daily Holidays

1. Antarctica Day, *Basketball Day, *Bifocals at the Monitor Liberation Day, Canada: Yukon Order of Pioneers (1894), *Civil Air Patrol Day, Portugal: Independence Day, Romania: National Holiday, Rosa Parks Day, Special Kids Day, *United Nations: World AIDS Day
2. *Artificial Heart Transplant Day (1967), *Joseph Bell (1837), England: Walter Plinge Day, Laos: National Day, National Mutt Day — December, *Special Education Day, United Arab Emirates: Independence Day, *United Nations: International Day for the Abolition of Slavery Day
3. Be a Blessing Day, E-Discovery Day, First Heart Transplant (1967), Ghana: National Farmers' Day, *United Nations: International Day of Persons with Disabilities
4. Bike Shop Day, Mary Celeste Discovery Day, National Grange Day, Saint Barbara's Day, Solar Eclipse (total), *Samuel Butler (1835)
5. *AFL–CIO Founded (1955), Austria: Krampuslauf, *Bathtub Party Day, Christmas to Remember Day, *Walt Disney (1901), Haiti: Discovery Day, "Irrational Exuberance" Day, Montgomery Bus Boycott Remembrance Day, *United Nations: International Volunteer Day for Economic and Social Development, United Nations: World Soil Day
6. Central African Republic: National Day (observed), Ecuador: Day of Quito: Founding (1534), Everglades National Park Established (1947), Finland: Independence Day, Missouri Earthquakes

(1811), *National Miners' Day, *National Pawnbrokers Day, *Saint Nicholas Day, Spain: Constitution Day
7. Armenian Earthquake (1988), Cote D'Ivoire: Commemoration Day, Giving Tuesday, Iran: Students Day, *National Fire Safety Council Day (1979), *National Pearl Harbor Remembrance Day, *United Nations: International Civil Aviation Day
8. AFL Day, Feast of Immaculate Conception, Guam: Lady of Camarin Day, Intermediate-Range Nuclear Forces Treaty (INF) Signed (1987), NAFTA Day, National Lard Day, Soviet Union Dissolved (1991), Uzbekistan: Constitution Day, *Eli Whitney (1765)
9. Birdseye Day, Tanzania: Independence and Republic Day, *United Nations: International Anti-Corruption Day, United Nations: International Day of Commemoration and Dignity of the Victims of the Crime of Genocide and of the Prevention of this Crime
10. *Dewey Decimal System Day, *Emily Dickinson (1830), Encyclopedia Britannica First Published (1879), *Thomas Hopkins Gallaudet (1787), *Human Rights Day, James Addams Day, *Ada Lovelace (1815), *Nobel Prize Awards Ceremonies, Official Lost and Found Day, Thailand: Constitution Day, *United Nations: Human Rights Day
11. Burkino Faso: Independence Day, Kaleidoscope Day, National Day of the Horse,*UNICEF Birthday, *United Nations: International Mountain Day
12. *Bonza Bottler Day™, Day of Our Lady of Guadalupe, Kenya: Jamhuri Day (Independence Day), Mexico: Guadalupe Day, *Poinsettia Day, *Puerto Rico: Las Mañanitas, Turkmenistan: Neutrality Day, United Nations: International Day of Neutrality, United Nations: International Universal Health Coverage Day
13. Malta: Republic Day, *New Zealand Discovery (1642), Sweden: Saint Lucia Day
14. Asarah B'Tevet, *Doolittle Day, Nostradamus (1503), South Pole Discovery (1911)
15. *Bill of Rights Day, *Cat Herders Day, Curaçao: Kingdom Day and Antillean Flag Day
16. *Jane Austen (1775), Bahrain: Independence Day, Bangladesh: Victory Day, *Barbie and Barney Backlash Day, *Ludwig Van Beethoven (1770), Boston Tea Party Day, Kazakhstan: Independence Day, Philippines: Philippine Christmas Observance and Simbang Gabi, South Africa: Reconciliation Day, *United Nations: Revokes Resolution on Zionism (1991)
17. *Aztec Calendar Stone Discovery Day (1790), *Clean Air Day, First Flight Anniversary Celebration Day, *Joseph Henry (1797), Libby Day, Take a New Year's Resolution to Stop Smoking (TANYRSS) Day, Underdog Day, *Wright Brothers Day
18. *Benjamin O Davis, Jr. (1912), *Joseph Grimaldi (1778), Mexico: Feast of Our Lady of Solitude, Niger: Republic Day, "To Tell the Truth" Day, United Nations: Arabic Language Day, *United Nations: International Migrants Day
19. Titanic Day
20. American Poet Laureate Day, Montgomery Bus Boycott Ends (1956), *Mudd Day, *United Nations: International Human Solidarity Day
21. *Heinrich Böll (1917), Celebrate Short Fiction Day, Benjamin Disraeli Birth (1804), *Crossword Puzzle Day, *Forefathers Day, *Humbug Day, *Phileas Fogg Win a Wager Day, Pilgrim Landing, Shorts Day, United Kingdom Allows Same-Sex Civil Partnerships Day, Yalda, Yule
22. Be a Lover of Silence Day, First Gorilla Born in Captivity (1956), Oglethorpe Day, *Giacomo Puccini (1858)
23. *Federal Reserve System (1913), Festivus, First Non-stop Flight Around the World (1987), Metric Conversion Act (1975), Mexico: Feast of Radishes, *Transistor Day (1947)
24. Austria: "Silent Night, Holy Night", *Christmas Eve, First Surface-to-Surface Guided Missile, *James Prescott Joule (1818), Libya: Independence Day

25. *A'Phabet Day or No-L-Day, *Christmas Day, Cuba: Christmas Returns, Taiwan: Constitution Day, Washington Crosses the Delaware (1776)
26. *Bahamas: Junkanoo, Boxing Day, Ireland: Day of the Wren, Luxembourg: Blessing of the Wine, National Candy Cane Day, *National Whiner's Day, Radium Discovery Day, Saint Stephen's Day, Second Day of Christmas, Slovenia: Independence Day, South Africa: Day of Goodwill
27. "Howdy Doody" Day, *Johannes Kepler (1571), *Louis Pasteur (1822), Saint John Feast Day
28. Australia: Proclamation Day, *Cinema Day, Endangered Species Day, *Holy Innocents Day or Childermas, *Pledge of Allegiance Day
29. Andrew Johnson Wreath-Laying, Saint Thomas of Canterbury: Feast Day, *Tick Tock Day, *YMCA Day
30. *Falling Needles Family Fest Day, *Rudyard Kipling (1865), "Let's Make a Deal" Day, Philippines: Rizal Day, USSR DAY (1922)
31. *First Nights, First US Bank Opens (1781), *Japan: Namahage, *Leap Second Adjustment Time Day, *Make Up Your Mind Day, *New Year's Eve, No Interruptions Day, Saint Sylvester's Day, Scotland: Hogmany

Holiday Marketing Ideas

Honor Your Pharmacists Month — Your hardworking pharmacist is often overlooked. But not today. This is their day to shine. Your pharmacists are an integral part of your health care team ensuring the safe and effective use of medications. So, this month to thank them for all they do why not show them an ounce of cure. Let them know you appreciate them in some small but significant way. Oh, and be sure to use the official APhM hashtags: #APhM2020 and #pharmacistsmonth when you post on social media.

Dec 1 Bifocals at the Monitor Liberation Day — While this holiday is about glasses, specifically bifocals, I read 'liberation' in the title and think how that could be the focus of today's celebration. Whether you are a bifocal wearer or not, trying to read the computer with just the right head tilt can cause eyestrain and fatigue. So, you also have rest and relaxation or stress relief as topics you could embrace. Tips on how to accomplish any of these topics shared with your customers and clients are easy to post on social media. Events are even better, though as your brand will have a much deeper reach as you join with your speakers to promote your event. So, do consider hosting an event rather than simply spending time on social media.

Dec 8 National Lard Day — Whether you think food or fat there's got to be a good way to promote your business on a Weird & Wacky holiday called National Lard Day. Everything from food drives to exercise, recipes to relaxation all could fit nicely as topics for inspiration today. Sharing any of these as advice, tips, or techniques with your customers and clients in emails or social media posts is advisable. However, to make it more enjoyable and thus more memorable, consider creating a Facebook live video of you sharing your thoughts. If we are allowed to meet in person again, consider a live event rather than online. Food tastings and recipe swaps, exercise techniques and custom diet plans are all recipes for success. At the very least, post a graphic on social media that you have branded to your business that others can (and will want to) share. You'll find one I created in the Samples Appendix in two different orientations. And as you would expect, your hashtag of the day is #NationalLardDay.

Dec 17 Clean Air Day — Is it a coincidence that Clean Air Day falls on the same day as TANYRSS Day? Stopping smoking would most assuredly improve the air around you. However, since our focus is the former let's discover a way or two you can use this holiday to market your business.

According to CleanAirDay.org examples of clean air events that can be done virtually include leading a class through an online science experiment, hosting a lunch and learn with a guest speaker to talk about the latest trends in clean air technology, a subject-specific tweet-storm, a webinar on bicycle safety, and much more. And examples of live events include bike-rides, giveaways, tree planting events, and public awareness efforts.

If you choose to host any of these types of events connect with other businesses in your area to make it a media blitz for the entire team. As the host organizer you are sure to be called upon by your local media and we all know the value of a little airtime.

Dec 26 National Candy Cane Day — Now that Christmas is behind us and the new year looming, it's time bit of frivolity. Enter the delicious candy cane. It comes in all shapes, sizes, and flavors. But is a straight candy cane really a candy 'cane'? The jury is still out on that point. Nevertheless, to make this sweet treat a notable marketing tool you could pass out canes with your business card or branded graphic attached to it to everyone you meet. Another alternative is to post candy cane facts throughout the day on your social media channels. If you look in the Samples Appendix, you'll find both a graphic and a few facts you can put to good use today. You'll also find there a few recipes that feature this sweet treat, some of them are even kid friendly, that you can use and share.

Appendix A: SAMPLES

Sample Press Release

FOR IMMEDIATE RELEASE

30+ YEAR LOCAL VETERAN BUSINESS OWNER / AUTHOR PARTNERS WITH PNC BANK

CLEARWATER, FL— SEPTEMBER 21, 2014
Local author and publisher, Ginger Marks, partners with Clearwater's PNC Bank to provide insight and advice for prospective, new, and experienced business owners. Ginger will be available to chat and sign copies of her award-winning book, Complete Library of Entrepreneurial Wisdom and PNC Financial experts will be on hand to field your questions and educate you on business financial matters.

Mrs. Marks has spent 30+ years in the Tampa Bay area honing her skill as an entrepreneur. Having owned and operated multiple businesses, including a restaurant and a multimillion-dollar surgical clinic, she knows her way around business and how to operate one successfully.

Mrs. Marks states, "Owning a business takes many talents and the determination to succeed. In the course of my business operations I have experienced both the ups and the downs of the financial market. Without the knowledge of how to structure your finances to support your dreams you endanger your success. This is why I have partnered with PNC with the release of this important work."

Event date and location: October 9, 2014 between 5:30 and 6:30 pm at 2498 Gulf-to-Bay Blvd. Books available at your local bookstore and at this event.

\# \# \#

MEDIA CONTACT: Ginger Marks, ginger.marks@documeantdesings.com 1 – 727 – 565 – 8500.

Random Act of Kindness Card

To brand these RAK card add your contact information below the dotted line.

National JoyGerm Day Graphics

Extraterrestrial Culture Day Social Media Graphic

To brand this card add your logo and contact information on the lower left above the date line.

Simplify Your Life Tips

The following tips can be used on your social media or you can make cute graphics if you are up to the task.

- Clean out your sock drawer. Get rid of all of them that have holes, are faded or worn, and also those mismatched ones you were hoping to find a mate to.
- Limit your time on social media … unless that is your job 😊.
- Place that call you've been meaning to place.
- Fire a client who is causing you stress.
- Run a defrag on your computer
- Empty out a drawer and throw away anything you don't need anymore.
- Clean out your closet, if you haven't worn it in ages, put it in a pile to give to Hospice.
- Uninstall unused computer programs on your computer.
- Clean out your spice cabinet. After a year it's time to throw out the old and start fresh.
- Take just three to five minutes to clean out a spot in your office of home.
- Schedule an appointment that you have been putting off.
- Use that gift certificate you got last year for your birthday or Christmas.
- Unsubscribe to unwanted newsletters that you no longer read.
- Organize all your passwords in one place. I have an Internet address & password logbook that I use. You can get one to help you too. The ISBN# is 978-14413-0814-6.
- Unclutter a single shelf in your office or home. Just one!
- Go through your CD/DVD collection and donate those that you probably won't watch again.
- Hire an assistant to do the mundane tasks you hate doing.
- Make a TODO list with the most uninspiring task at the top. Then check them off as you do them. If you don't finish all in one day, start where you left off the following day.
- Put a couple of garbage bag liners underneath the one you are using. This makes it easy to replace when the time comes.
- Fold your bedsheets, fresh from the laundry, so that they can easily be unfolded as you put them on your bed. Tip, if you fold them inside out, they will be easier to unfold onto your mattress.

Balloon Piggy Bank

Courtesy of Enchanted Learning and Crafts

Allow plenty of time between steps for drying. If you don't have that kind of time, perhaps you could make the bodies ahead and let the kids put the finishing touches on.

SUPPLIES NEEDED:

One balloon for each piggy bank
A lot of old newspaper and/or brown-bag paper A paper egg carton (plastic ones won't work) or bathroom cups Cardboard
Masking tape
Flour-water glue (instructions below)
Pink paint (tempera works well) and a brush or pink tissue paper One pink pipe cleaner A craft knife
Plastic googly eyes (optional)
Markers

Flour-water Glue for Paper-Maché: Make a simple, thin glue from flour and water (boiling gives it a nice consistency). Mix 1 cup of flour into 1 cup of water until the mixture is thin and runny. Stir into 4 cups of boiling water. Simmer for about 3 minutes, then cool.

Blow up a balloon for each piggy bank.

Have the child tear a lot of strips of newspaper and/or brown bag paper. Strips should be about 1 inch or less wide; the length doesn't really matter. Time crunched, tear these ahead of time. Dip each strip of paper in the flour glue and wrap around the balloon. Have at least two to three layers surrounding the balloon. Let it dry (at least overnight) after each layer.

Let the papier-mâché balloon dry for a few days. When it is dry, you can pop and remove the balloon from the inside. This will be the body and head of the pig.

After the papier-mâché is completely dry, it's time to add the legs, ears, and the snout. Separate 5 paper egg carton sections (one for each leg and the snout) or small paper cups. (Cut the fifth cup down to 1-inch and tape to the front for a snout.) Cut two triangles for ears out of the cardboard. Tape them in place for ears. Use the masking tape to attach them to the oval-shaped body.

To color your pig, either paint it with tempera paint or use pink tissue paper.

For the tissue paper coating, first tear or cut the tissue paper into small pieces (a few inches in all directions). Then cover the pig with a very thin layer of the flour-water glue (using your fingers is the easiest way). Next, put the tissue paper pieces on the pig (you may need to add a little more glue occasionally) until you have a nice pink coat for the pig.

Let the pig dry completely (at least overnight).

The tail: Using a sharp crafts knife, make a small hole at the tail end of the pig. Insert a pipe cleaner into the hole, then shape the pipe cleaner into a spiral.

Eyes: Make eyes with a marker or glue on plastic googly eyes.

Nostrils: Make two nostrils on the snout with a marker.

The Money Slot: Along the top of the pig's body, carefully cut a slot large enough to fit any coin.

20 Famous Pigs

1. Porky Pig
2. Miss Piggy
3. Piglet
4. Babe
5. 3 Little Pigs
6. Wilbur
7. Arnold Ziffel
8. Petunia
9. Hamm
10. Mr. Porky
11. Petunia Pig
12. Plopper
13. Pig
14. This Little Piggie
15. Annie Sue
16. Gordy
17. Red
18. Piglet
19. Gub-Gub
20. Paddington

National Pig Day Graphics

Dress in Blue Graphic

Dress in Blue Day May 5, 2021

Healthy Colon Habits
- Get screened if you are over 45 or high risk
- Monitor your weight
- Quit smoking
- Reduce stress
- Exercise to strengthen your digestive tract
- Listen to your body!

Tips to Promote a Healthy Colon
- Limit red meat
- Reduce or eliminate processed meats
- Reduce excess sugar
- Eliminate fried foods
- Trade starchy foods with vegetables
- Limit alcohol consumption to one or two per day

Pecan Recipes

Cinnamon Pecans

Ingredients
1 cup white sugar
1 teaspoon salt
1 teaspoon ground cinnamon
1 egg white
1 tablespoon water
1-pound pecan halves

Directions
In a large bowl stir together first three ingredients. Set aside.

In a small bowl whip the egg white with the water until foamy.

Add the egg white foamy egg white to the large bowl and mix lightly.

Add the pecans to the mixture and stir to coat.

Transfer the pecans onto a cookie sheet in a single layer. Bake for 1 hour in a 250-degree oven stirring every 15 minutes.

Store in an airtight container.

Pecan Sandies

Ingredients
1 cup margarine, softened
1 cup vegetable oil
1 cup white sugar
1 cup confectioners' sugar, sifted
2 eggs
1 teaspoon vanilla extract
4 cups all-purpose flour
1 teaspoon baking soda
1 teaspoon cream of tartar
1 teaspoon salt
2 cups chopped pecans
½ cup white sugar for decoration

Directions
Preheat oven to 375 degrees F (190 degrees C).

In a large bowl, cream together the margarine, vegetable oil, 1 cup white sugar and confectioners' sugar until smooth. Beat in the eggs one at a time, then stir in the vanilla. Combine the flour, baking soda, cream of tartar and salt; stir into the creamed mixture. Mix in the pecans. Roll dough into 1-inch balls and roll each ball in remaining white sugar. Place the cookies 2 inches apart onto ungreased cookie sheets.

Bake for 10 to 12 minutes in the preheated oven, or until the edges are golden. Remove from cookie sheets to cool on wire racks.

© Copyright 2020 allrecipes.com. All rights reserved. https://www.allrecipes.com.

Divinity

Ingredients
2-2/3 cups sugar
2/3 cup light corn syrup
½ cup water*
2 egg whites
1 teaspoon vanilla
2/3 cup pecans pieces

Directions
Stir sugar, corn syrup, and water over low heat until sugar is dissolved. Cook, without stirring to 260 degrees on a candy thermometer (or until a small amount of mixture dropped into very cold water forms a hard ball).

In mixer bowl, beat egg whites until stiff peaks form. Continue beating while pouring hot syrup in a thin stream into egg whites. Add vanilla; beat until mixture holds its shape and becomes slightly dull. (Mixture may become too stiff for mixer.) Fold in nuts. Drop mixture from tip of buttered spoon onto waxed paper.

Yield: about 4 dozen candies. *Use 1 tablespoon less water on humid days.

Pecan Pralines

Ingredients
1 cup granulated sugar
1 cup brown sugar (packed)
1/2 cup heavy cream*
1/4 teaspoon salt
2 tablespoons butter*
1 cup pecan halves

Directions
Lightly butter of aluminum foil. Combine sugars, cream, and salt in a large saucepan. Cook over medium heat, stirring constantly, to 228 degrees on a candy thermometer (or until the mixture spins a thread about 2 inches long when dropped from a spoon).

Stir in butter and pecans. Continue cooking, stirring constantly, to 236 degrees (or until a small amount of the mixture dropped into very cold water forms a soft ball which flattens when removed from the water). Remove from heat; cool 5 minutes.

Beat the mixture with a wooden spoon until slightly thickened and candy just coats nuts but does not lose its glossy appearance. Drop candy by large spoonfuls onto buttered foil.

Yield: about 1-1/2 dozen candies.

*I use heavy cream and real butter for a creamier praline. However, you can use margarine and 20% light cream if you are watching calories. But, if that's the case, why are you even making them (giggle)?

Pecan Fingers

Ingredients
2/4 cup shortening (half butter or margarine, softened)
3/4 cup confectioners' sugar
1-1/2 cups all-purpose flour*
2 eggs
1 cup brown sugar (packed)
2 tablespoons flour
1/2 teaspoon baking powder
1/2 teaspoon salt
1/2 teaspoon vanilla
1 cup chopped pecans

Directions
Heat oven to 350 degrees. Cream shortening and confectioners' sugar. Blend in 1-1/2 cups flour. Press evenly in bottom of ungreased 13x9x2-inch baking pan. Bake 12 to 15 minutes.

Mix remaining ingredients; spread over hot baked layer and back 20 minutes longer. Cool; cut into 3x1 inch bars.

Yield: 32 cookies. *Self-rising flour can be used in this recipe.

Pecan Pie Bars
By Cindy Rahe

Pecan Pie Bars are easy to make for the holidays, easy to transport, and even easier to eat. They're just like pecan pie, but no need for the knife and fork!

Ingredients
For the shortbread crust:
2 cups (9oz/255g) all-purpose flour
1/2 cup (3.5oz/100g) granulated sugar
3/4 teaspoon salt
3/4 cup (6oz/170g) unsalted butter cut into pieces

For the pecan filling:
2 cups chopped pecans
3/4 cup (3.5oz/100g) dark brown sugar
2 tablespoons all-purpose flour
Pinch of salt
4 large eggs
2 teaspoons vanilla bean paste or extract
1 cup light corn syrup
Extra pecan halves, for placing on top of the bars

Directions

Preheat the oven to 375-degrees F and grease and line an 8x8-inch square baking pan (metal or glass) with parchment. Make sure to line at least the bottom and two sides so you can easily lift the bars from the pan.

I use a large piece of parchment (pre-cut for a sheet pan) and fit the whole thing into the baking pan, folding in the corners, so I can lift out the bars in one piece and not have to deal with any sticky filling baking onto the sides or bottom of the pan.

Make the crust: Pulse the flour, sugar, salt, and butter into a food processor until combined. The mixture will be sandy.

Continue to process the mixture until it goes from sandy to clumpy. When this starts to happen the food processor will actually sound different. It will be less high-pitched and have more of a low rumble sound.

Bake the crust: Once the crust mixture clumps up, transfer it from the food processor to the prepared pan. Press it firmly and evenly in the bottom of the pan.

Pierce the crust all over with a fork and bake in the oven for 30 to 35 minutes or until light to medium golden brown all over.

Prepare the filling: Add the chopped pecans to a mixing bowl and set aside. Using the same food processor bowl used to make the crust (no need to clean it out), combine the brown sugar, flour, salt, eggs, vanilla bean paste, and corn syrup (add the corn syrup last so it doesn't get stuck on the bottom of the food processor).

Pulse until completely combined. Pour the mixture over the chopped pecans and fold to combine.

Bake the bars: Once the crust is baked, remove it from the oven and reduce the heat to 350°F. Scrape the pecan mixture onto the baked crust. Place an extra few pecan halves on the top of the filling as decoration.

Return the pan to the oven and bake for 35 to 40 minutes, until the center is just set. If the center still jiggles, bake for a few more minutes; if you notice the bars starting to puff in the middle, remove them immediately.

Cool and serve: Cool the bars on a rack completely before lifting from the pan. Cut into 2x2-inch squares and serve. These bars can be stored in an airtight container at room temperature for 2 to 3 days.

Yields 16 square bars.

The Grass is Always Browner on the Other Side of the Fence Day Social Media Graphic

Blah! Blah! Blah! Day Social Media Graphic

Public Schools Day Social Media Graphic

Hat Etiquette

Courtesy of LifeHacker.com.au

When It's Okay to Wear a Hat

Generally, it's okay to wear your hat when you're outside, on the street, or in public areas, regardless of whether you're a man or woman. It is possible for some of these public areas to be inside, though. For example, it's okay to wear your hat indoors at places like hotel lobbies, airports, train stations, long indoor corridors, elevators, public transportation and so on.

Ladies, you can wear hats—as long as it isn't a baseball cap—just about anywhere outdoors and indoors, including during some meals (especially if they're outdoors). If you're wearing a baseball cap, however, you must follow the same rules that apply to men's hats.

When to Take Your Hat Off

Guys, whether you're wearing a fedora, trilby, or a baseball cap, you shouldn't be wearing your hat indoors most of the time (again, some public areas are okay). For example, places where hats are always off-limits include homes, schools, restaurants, cafes, churches, theatres, and some businesses (especially if you're there for business). But even if you are in an area where hats are OK, you should take them off in the presence of a lady. You should also remove your hat during meals, during movies, during the national anthem, during weddings, during funerals, during dedications, while taking photographs, and when you're being introduced to someone.

Ladies, the only time you must remove your hat is when it might block someone's view or cause an inconvenience to others. So, you shouldn't wear a hat at the theatre, or while you're working. It should be noted that you can also wear your hat during the national anthem, during some meals, and when you're introduced to someone. But again, if it's a baseball cap, you should follow the same guidelines as men.

Etiquette Tips

- When you remove your hat, hold it in your hand so the inner lining is never visible.
- When removing your hat to introduce yourself or say hello, a simple slight lifting of the hat off your head for a moment will do. Accompany the gesture with a nod and a smile.
- Alternatively, you can tip your hat by grabbing the brim and pulling down ever so slightly. If you've ever seen a Western, you've probably seen cowboys do this a lot. It's less formal than pulling the hat off your head, but still a polite gesture.
- If your hat has any ornamentation—feathers, pins and so on—men should always have it on the left side of the hat. For women, the ornament should be on the right side of the hat.

National Odometer Day Event Flyer

International Learn to Swim Day Social Media Graphic

"Tear Down This Wall" Day Social Media Graphic

National Prune Day Health Benefits

- A good source of energy, and they don't cause a rapid hike in blood sugar levels
- High in fiber, which can help you regulate your bowels and your bladder
- Helps digestion
- Contain fiber, which can prevent constipation and hemorrhoids
- Nature's laxative
- Good source of potassium. This mineral helps with digestion, heart rhythm, nerve impulses, and muscle contractions, as well as blood pressure.
- High in vitamins K, A, riboflavin, B-6, and niacin
- Contain high amounts of minerals such as manganese, copper, and magnesium
- Good source of iron
- Builds muscle and bone
- Reduces cholesterol
- Lowers blood pressure
- Helps reduce your appetite by keeping you feeling full longer since they are slow to digest
- Protects against emphysema
- Lowers risk of colon cancer

National Prune Day Social Media Graphic

National Lighthouse Day Social Media Graphic

10 Health Benefits of Chocolate

Courtesy of https://10faq.com/

1. Lowers blood pressure
2. Encourages weight loss by reducing our cravings
3. Hydrates the skin by improving blood flow
4. A good source of copper, iron, magnesium, manganese, and potassium and healthy fats that may be able to reduce the risk of heart disease
5. Relaxes blood vessels which improves blood flow through the entire system
6. Reduces the risk of heart disease
7. Improves cognitive function
8. Reduces oxidation, which helps to protect our cells against damage
9. Relieves the levels of stress hormones
10. Helps the body to regulate blood sugar levels

National Dog Day Social Media Graphic

Organize a Food Drive

Courtesy of AARP

Step 1: PICK A LOCAL GROUP THAT NEEDS FOOD

Consider both the obvious (food bank and homeless shelter) and the less obvious (faith-based organizations, senior citizen centers, schools).

If you want suggestions on food organizations in need, start by contacting your local food bank. You'll find them listed online at http://www.FeedingAmerica.org.

Food banks are warehouses that collect large quantities of food to distribute to local food pantries, soup kitchens, etc. The food bank itself may be interested in benefiting from your drive. Or, they may suggest a local food organization in your neighborhood.

Once you've determined which organization will benefit from your drive, use the questions on the enclosed Tip Sheet as a guide to help adapt the Food Drive to their needs.

Local food organizations often are in short supply of age-appropriate food (e.g., low sodium, low sugar, or easy to open foods) and/or culturally-appropriate foods. Find sample lists of these foods in this how-to guide and consider narrowing your requests for donations to these special foods.

If no local organization needs support, consider making a donation to help those who are hungry. Each day millions face the impossible choice between buying food or the medicines they need. AARP Foundation provides assistance to vulnerable seniors and older adults struggling to make ends meet. Help us fight senior hunger and support critical programs that help individuals in need by making a tax-deductible contribution.

Step 2: IT'S A SNAP!

Another way to help hungry families buy the food they need is to encourage them to apply for SNAP (Supplemental Nutritional Assistance Program—formerly called food stamps). Consider handing out the flyer in this packet to promote SNAP. You could ask the food bank if they would like assistance in promoting this program. If so, you can hand out flyers during your food drive, and/or leave flyers in places of faith, senior centers, grocery stores, etc.

Each state's SNAP application process and form is different, so there is room at the bottom of the sample flyer for you to print the local agency or state agency's phone number. Visit www.aarp.org/snapmap to look up the phone numbers. Find more information about how to help others with SNAP on www.CreateTheGood.org/how-to.

Step 3: DECIDE HOW YOU WANT TO COLLECT FOOD

- Single-site drop off: Ask people to bring food donations to one location during set hours on a specific day. Volunteers man the collection site.
- Extended food drive: Set up numerous collection points with drop boxes where people can leave food over the course of numerous weeks. Volunteers collect the donations once per day.
- Event-related food drive: Your team partners with a local event—like a sports game, music festival or county fair—and sets up collection sites at the event.

Got a community garden? Consider arranging donations from the garden to the recipient organization. Rules vary on accepting fresh food, so be sure to talk this over with the organization you have in mind. Interested in starting a community garden? Check out the how-to guide on www.CreateTheGood.org/how-to.

Step 4: ASSESS VOLUNTEER NEEDS

Establish a small committee to plan and coordinate the food drive. Select an overall coordinator (that may be you) and team leaders for individual tasks. Depending on the size of your food drive, there could be 2 to 6 team leaders.

Schedule a training session for the team leads. Provide the leads with background on the selected organizations, a list of key dates/times (timeline of preparation), responsibilities needed to carry out the food drive and contact information for you and the other team leads.

The team leads should:
- Help recruit volunteers for the food drive
- Promote the food drive with flyers throughout the community
- Ensure local media are aware of the drive
- Set up the collection site
- Lead a shift during the event
- Help coordinate food sorting and delivery after the drive.

Step 5: FIND A DROP-OFF LOCATION

Identify the desired location for food drop-off and collection such as a school, local business, shopping center, faith-based organization, or grocery store.

Contact the appropriate person (store manager, principal, etc.) to get permission to hold the drive there and ask if they'd like to participate in any way. When you call, make sure you have information on the food drive (the goal, the preferred date, background on the organization the food will support, etc.).

Depending on the size of the drive and the number of volunteers, you might want to hold it at multiple locations. Keep in mind this requires more logistical organization and volunteers but will yield more food.

Once you nail down a location, work out logistics with your contact there:
- Where specifically the food drive can be held (e.g., at the entrance of the store or a section of the parking lot)
- The date and hours of operation for the drive
- Inclement weather backup plan
- Where the food will be stored before pick-up
- Place to accommodate the volunteers who will organize the food for pick up.

NOTE: If you are talking to a retailer and they are interested, you might explore additional ways they could support the effort. Examples might include:

- Printing your flyers (the retailer could receive an acknowledgment on the flyer)
- Matching the donations raised from the public for the food drive in some way (with a dollar amount or a product donation from the retailer to the food bank or organization).
- Encouraging customers to donate money at the cash register for the food organization.

Step 6: RECRUIT VOLUNTEERS

Ask your family, friends, colleagues, neighbors, and faith group members to help make the food drive a success. Check with the local community organizations, libraries, schools, senior citizen centers, places of worship, etc. that may already have a pool of volunteers for their own purposes. Email is a great way to keep the volunteers informed.

See the Tip Sheet in this guide for suggestions on how to manage volunteers.

Post the food drive on Create the Good to recruit more volunteers or to promote the drive.

Step 7: GET THE WORD OUT

The key to a successful food drive is to get the word out about the event. Promote! Promote! Promote!

See the tip sheet in this guide for suggestions on how to publicize your event.

Step 8: FINAL ARRANGEMENTS

Confirm all details with the recipient organization, your team leaders, and your contact person at the drive location to:

- Dropping off boxes/crates prior to the drive and picking up food following the drive
- Food sorting instructions (if any)
- Supplying tables, chairs, and refreshments for the volunteers
- Staffing schedule for the day of the food drive (2 to 3-hour shifts are best)
- Creating and posting 3 or 4 large signs within a block or two of the food drive on event day.
- Be prepared with information for people that tell you they need food. Identify the closest food pantry, as well as the closest place people can go to get assistance in applying for SNAP, the food stamp program (see SNAP flyer in this kit).

Step 9: EVENT DAY

Set up the food collection site (i.e., two tables with chairs behind it; refreshments behind the volunteer chairs, boxes/crates clearly labeled for various food types).

- Post the Food Drive signs in visible areas and have flyers available.
- Welcome volunteers as they arrive and show them how things will work.
- Relax, smile, and enjoy the wonderful event that is bringing together the community.
- When the drive is over, clean up the area, and take down the signs. Leave the area the same (if not cleaner) than when you arrived.
- Thank the hosting organization and the volunteers.

Step 10: FOLLOW UP (within one week after the event)
- Send a thank you note, call or email to all volunteers (using the method by which they prefer to be contacted). Include how much food was donated and whether there are plans for additional food drives or other volunteer opportunities.
- Call or write a thank you note to the hosting organization. Again, let them know how much food was donated and convey their important role in the success of the program and the difference they are making.
- While it is still fresh in your mind, develop a list of lessons learned for future events. Check in with the local food organization to see if they have suggestions to include.
- Keep in touch with volunteers and local communities for future volunteer opportunities.

Step 11: INSPIRE OTHERS ON CREATETHEGOOD.ORG
Tell us what you did!

We want to hear stories about how you helped give back to your community at www.CreateTheGood.org/stories. You just might inspire others to do the same.

Share Feedback

We are always looking for feedback on our materials, so please let us know how this guide was helpful or additional information you wish we could have included. Share lessons learned and other tips for others who are organizing food drives at www.aarp.org/CreateTheGoodgroup.

Keep up the good!

Remember, whether you've got five minutes, five hours, or five days, you can make a positive impact in your community. And if you have more time, consider organizing another service activity, finding local opportunities and posting your events at www.CreateTheGood.org.

Tip Sheet: Meeting an Organization's Needs
Once you have selected the local program you would like to support, get more information on their needs before you start implementing a comprehensive plan. Don't be afraid to ask lots of questions. You'll want to be armed with information for your volunteers! Here are some suggested areas to discuss:
- Who is the best contact person for the food drive?
- What are the best times of year and dates to receive food donations?
- What types of food are in short supply? What specific foods may be needed?
- Healthy, age-appropriate food (e.g. low-sodium or low-sugar foods, and/or easy-to-open packages?
- Culturally-appropriate products? (needs will vary by local population)
- Non-food items?
- Specific foods or packaging that they cannot accept?
- Acceptance of fresh food?
- Preference for quantities of each food type (e.g., large or small packages)

- How should the food be sorted at the collection site (e.g., canned food, boxed food, condiments, etc.)?
- Does the organization have boxes or crates for food sorting?
- How will the food be delivered to the organization (pick-up or delivery?)
- When is the best time for pickup and delivery?
- Can they provide information on the organization for volunteers, donors, or media outlets?

Tips on Managing Volunteers

Develop a roster of all the volunteers. Be sure to get their full name and contact information so you can keep them informed during the planning stage.

Host a meeting three to five weeks prior to the food drive so the volunteers understand the goal of the food drive, what is required of them, the timeline of the drive and background on the selected organization you are supporting. Provide a take-away sheet with the information provided at the meeting.

Develop a schedule for the volunteers so that you have sufficient support throughout the day. Communicate the schedule to all the volunteers two weeks prior to the food drive so there is time for rescheduling if needed. Suggested tasks for volunteers include:
- Make and distribute flyers/signs for event promotion
- Promote the event through personal contacts and local community organizations (see specifics in Generating Publicity Tip Sheet). Staff the event (including set up and take down)
- Transport food donations to the recipient organization
- Follow up communications, including the food drive results and thanking the supporters

For more tips on project management, see the Nuts and Bolts Guide for Organizers at www.CreateTheGood.org/how-to.

Tips on Generating Publicity

Make a Flyer

Be creative but also provide key information. You may want to look at other organizations' food drive flyers for ideas. Included on the flyer should be:
- Suggested foods for contribution (specific items requested by the organizations, non- perishable foods, gift cards)
- Date, time, and location of the event
- Brief information on the organization that will receive the food Look at other food drive flyers to get ideas
- Pertinent contact information for more information

Distribute the Flyer

Consider the same sources used for recruiting volunteers (schools, faith-based organizations, community centers) and public places including grocery stores, coffee shops, libraries, etc.

Word of Mouth Goes a Long Way

- Spread the word to your friends, family, neighbors, and co-workers. Talk to them in person or use email or social media (e.g., Facebook, Twitter) to get the word out. Ask them to spread the word as well.

- Approach everyone with a friendly, positive attitude. Explain that it will be a fun event focused on a great cause.

- Use message boards — both online and the old-fashioned way.

Reach the Largest Audience

Use your local newspapers, magazines, community guides, Web sites, radio stations, and television and cable access channels to help spread the word about your food drive to expand your audience. The local press often welcomes information about community events. And many radio and TV stations and news outlets offer online forms to simplify event promotion. Also try to get the details in school and faith-based newsletter or bulletin announcements.

How to Contact the Media

Ask some volunteers to develop a list of local editors and reporters (names, phone numbers and email addresses). Most newspapers and radio and television stations will list newsroom contact information on their websites. The reporters most interested in your announcement will be community editors.

- E-mail basic details of the event, using plain text without any fancy graphics.

- Put the event's date in the subject line. The e-mail should include:

- Name of event (_____ Food Drive)

- Complete date and time of the food drive

- What organization is being supported, and how much food you are hoping to assemble for a specific cause

- Any special guests or events

- Your contact information (for further questions and possible volunteers)

- Send your announcements at least two weeks before the food drive day.

- Follow up with reporters several days after the event to announce the results of the drive, the approximate number of donors and volunteers and where the food will go. Send this information to the same media list.

The best time to send media announcements are Tuesdays, Wednesdays, and Thursdays.

Publicizing the Food Drive–Before and After

Use the attached sample Promotional Flyer as a guide to create your own flyer.

Ask permission to display flyers, posters, or postcards at coffee shops, libraries, malls, and local businesses. Invite local businesses to participate with you.

Ask local community members to promote the food drive through their local place of faith, clubs, community groups, etc. People are most likely to do this if they're motivated by the charity that will benefit from the donations. Invite a local celebrity—a congressional representative, your mayor, or a radio show host—to highlight the need for food and promote the event.

Sample Food Drive Food List

Healthy Foods for All Ages

(Please check with your local food collection agency to determine the most needed items in your community, including fresh fruits and vegetables)

- Non-perishable Food Items
- Canned Proteins (tuna, salmon, chicken, peanut butter) peanuts, etc.
- Canned Fruits in Own Juices or Light Syrup (pineapples, peaches, and pears)
- 100% Fruit Juices (all sizes including juice boxes)
- Grains (pasta, whole wheat pasta, rice, brown rice, macaroni, and cheese) bags of beans: black, pink, kidney, etc.; corn flour or MASECA (for tortillas)
- Condiments (tomato-based sauces, light soy sauce, ketchup, mustard, light salad dressings) Goya powder condiments; salt; sugar (brown)
- Low Sodium/ No Salt Added Canned Vegetables (mixed, green beans, corn) beans: black, pink, kidney, etc.
- Soups (beef stew, chili, chicken noodle, turkey rice)
- Multigrain Cereal (Cheerios, Corn Flakes, Grape-Nuts, Raisin Bran)

Food Drive Flyer

Neighborhood Food Drive

create the good - AARP

NEIGHBORHOOD LOCATION: _____

Please partticipate in a neighborhood food drive on:
DATE: _____
TIME: _____

ITEMS NEEDED:

For more information, contact:

Name:

Phone Number:

Email Address:

SNAP Flyer

It's Worth The Time...

"It gives me money to go and buy meat...."

"...I had more money to buy food – and with the money I had leftover, I paid bills."

"I can buy things that I WANT to eat..."

...to get help paying for groceries.

Go to www.aarp.org/snap to learn how easy it is to apply for the new **S**upplemental **N**utritional **A**ssistance **P**rogram.

It's a SNAP.

AARP and AARP Foundation believe that no one of any age should go hungry.
Learn more about AARP's Hunger Campaign at
www.aarp.org/hunger

World Smile Day Social Media Graphic

WORLD SMILE DAY — OCTOBER 1

facts

- Boosts immune system
- Relieves stress by releasing endorphins
- It's easier to smile than frown
- It takes up to 53 muscles to smile
- We are born with the ability to smile
- There are 19 different types of smiles all with their own meaning

World Purse Day Social Media Image

Saxophone Day Graphic

National Lard Day Social Media Graphics

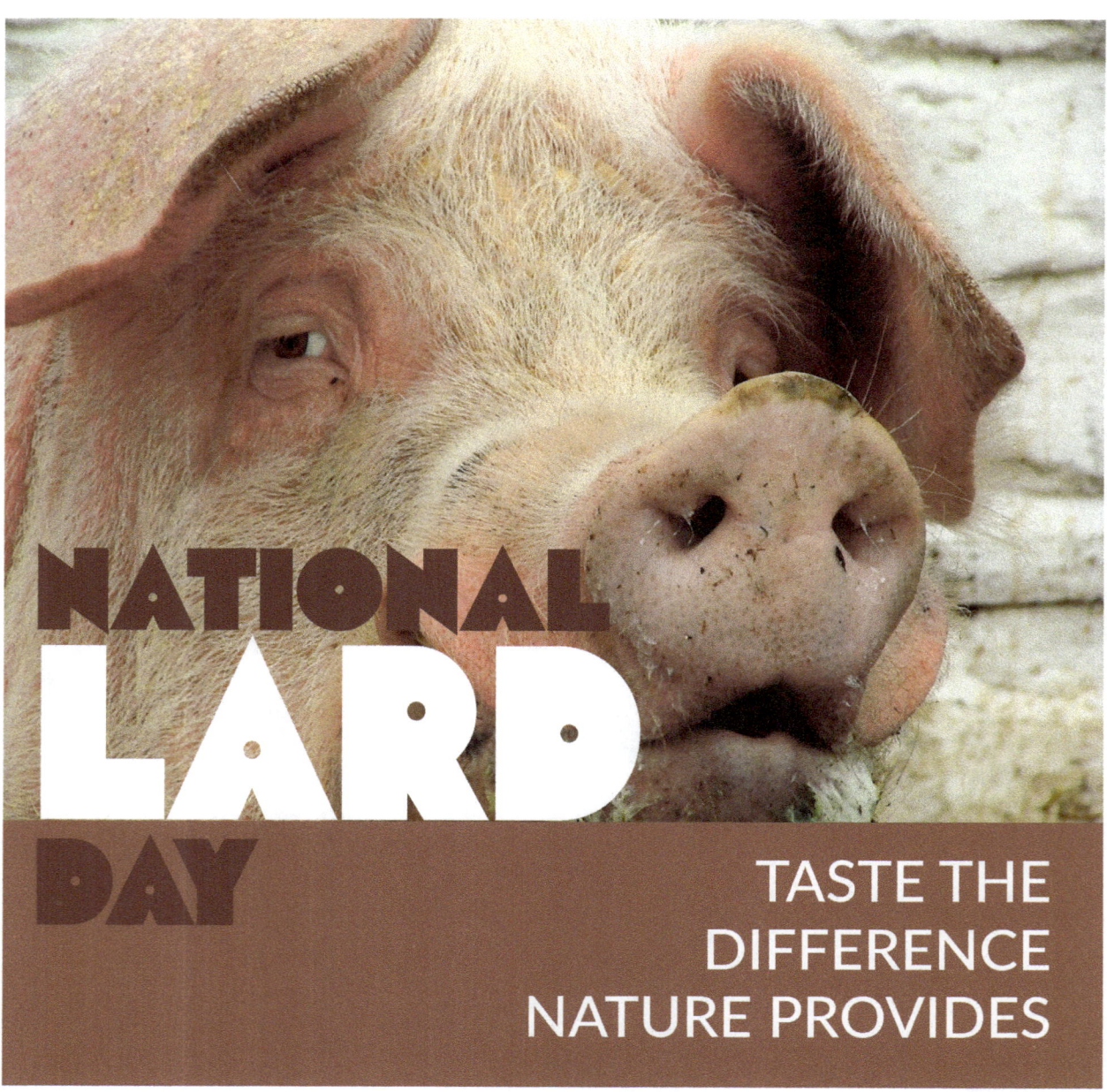

National Candy Cane Day Card

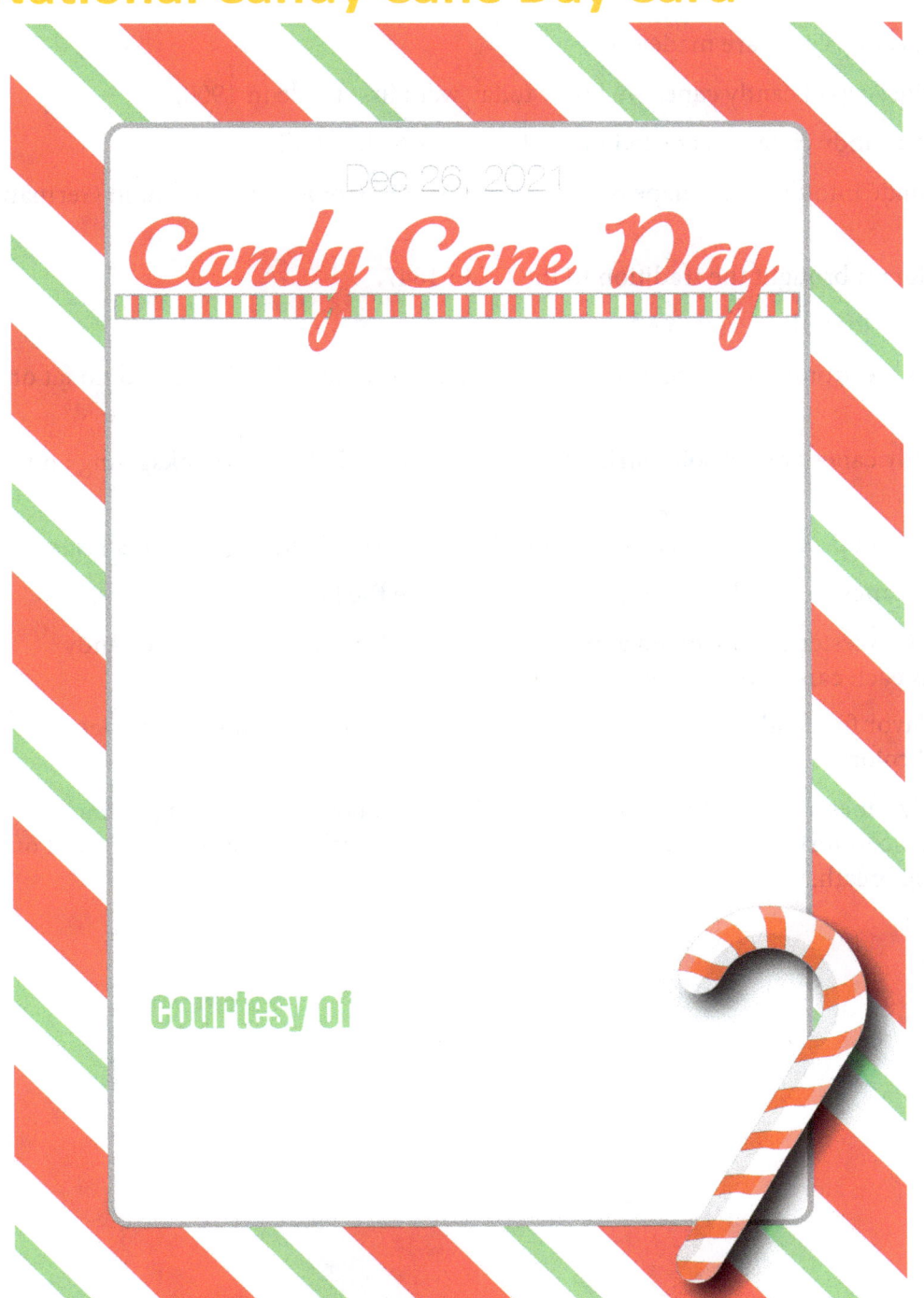

National Candy Cane Day Facts

- Over 1.76 billion candy canes are made every year.
- The red-and-white striped candy canes we know today were first made in 1900.
- The world's largest candy cane was created in 2011 and was 63 feet tall!
- They first were made into the cane shape by the choirmaster in Cologne Cathedral in Germany back in 1670.
- A German immigrant brought the tradition to the US in 1847.
- They weren't always striped.
- Most candy canes are around five inches long, containing only about 50 calories and no fat or cholesterol.
- 10 percent of candy canes are not sold during the holiday season between Thanksgiving and Christmas.
- A candy cane turned upside down reveals the letter J, which many believe represents Jesus.
- Originally, candy canes were only white, and they didn't have the bend.
- In 1921, Brasher O. Westerfield invented a machine that could automatically make candy canes. Before this each cane was made by hand.
- The traditional flavor for candy canes is peppermint, however, it is also made in a variety of other flavors and colors.
- Peppermint candy canes are touted for some substantial health benefits including aiding in gastrointestinal discomfort, curbing cravings, easing headaches, relieving stuffy noses, and of course, freshening breath.

Candy Cane Recipes

Courtesy of 123 Homeschool 4 Me https://www.123homeschool4me.com/

Candy Cane White Coconut Hot Cocoa
from Flour on My Face

Ingredients
3 Cups of Silk Coconut Milk
1 ¼ cups Ghirardelli Classic White Chocolate Chips
1 vanilla bean, split and scrapped or 1 tsp vanilla extract
½ cup Andes Peppermint Crunch chips or ¼- ½ tsp peppermint extract.

Directions
Add coconut milk, Ghirardelli Classic White Chocolate Chips, and vanilla bean to a heavy saucepan.

Heat until chocolate melts, whisking to keep the chocolate from sticking or burning on the bottom of the pan.

Whisk until the chocolate has melted and the cocoa is hot.

Add Andes Chips or peppermint extract (start with ¼ tsp and taste, then adjust).

Add vanilla extract if you didn't use a vanilla bean.

Pour into a mug, top with whipped cream. Garnish with a candy cane and a sprinkle of Andes Peppermint Crunch Chips or red and white sprinkles.

Candy Cane Lollipops
from 5 Minutes for Mom

For our lollipops, we simply positioned our candy canes onto lollipop sticks and poured on melted white chocolate to form the lollipops.

To melt the chocolate in a double boiler. Simply position a heat safe bowl on top of a pot of water on the stove and bring the water to a gentle boil. Don't allow the bowl to touch the water and stir the chocolate until melted.

If you want to form your lollipop hearts into a better heart shape, One Little Project and Sprinkle Some Sunshine! suggest you pop the candy canes and sticks in the oven for 3 minutes to soften the candy canes so you can mold them into heart shapes.

Candy Cane Bark
from Mess for Less

Ingredients
Candy canes (flavor of your choosing – we used cherry candy canes)
8 oz Bark mix
8 oz semi-sweet chocolate chips
Holiday sprinkles

Hammer (we used a meat tenderizer)
Parchment paper

Unwrap the candy canes and place a few in a zippered bag. For the amount of bark that we made, we used three candy canes. The next step is really fun for kids. Have them smash the bark into small pieces using a small hammer. When smashing the candy canes, be sure to leave some large chunks as well as smaller pieces.

Place a piece of parchment paper onto a cookie sheet. Melt the chocolate chips in the microwave and pour into the parchment paper covered cookie sheet. Spread the chocolate in an even layer. It will not cover the entire pan. You just want to create a square or rectangle of chocolate.

Next, melt the white chocolate in the microwave. Pour it on top of the semi-sweet chocolate. Spread it over the chocolate layer evenly until the chocolate layer is covered.

Now it's time to sprinkle the candy cane pieces on the bark. The kids had lots of fun with this step. We also added some festive holiday sprinkles to the bark. Press the candy cane pieces and sprinkles into the bark a bit so they will not fall out when it hardens.

Put the cookie sheet in the refrigerator for about an hour so that the bark could harden. Once it hardens, you can remove it from the parchment paper and break it into chunks.

Candy Cane Pretzel Candy
from See Mom Click

Ingredients
Waffle shaped square pretzels
Caramels (I used Kraft brand)
Candy Canes

Directions
Preheat the oven to 350 degrees Fahrenheit.

Put a piece of parchment paper on a baking tray. Place the pretzels on the tray in rows. I put about 15–20 on each sheet.

Cut the caramels in half through the thickness and place one half of a caramel on top of each pretzel.

Bake in the oven for about 5 minutes. I highly suggest watching these carefully on your first batch. Once they start to soften (you'll be able to tell when the corners start to round) it can go pretty quickly into a puddle after that. At 5 minutes mine were just soft enough without being runny. While they're in the oven put a couple of candy canes in a plastic baggie and break them up. I hit them a few times with the back of a wooden spoon. This is a good job for the kids!

When the caramels have softened, pull the tray out of the oven. Sprinkle candy cane pieces on top. You might want to give them a light push to get some stuck in the caramel.

As soon as they're cool enough to eat, go for it!

Store in an airtight container.

Candy Cane Oreo Santa Hat Cookies
from SnakWorks.com

Ingredients
4 oz. brick cream cheese, softened
2 Tbsp. sugar
1/2 cup thawed frozen whipped topping
20 OREO Cookies
20 strawberries, caps removed

Instructions
MIX cream cheese and sugar in small bowl until blended. Gently stir in whipped topping. Spoon into small resealable plastic bag; cut off 1 corner from bottom of bag.

PIPE cream cheese mixture onto cookies. Top with strawberries, bottom-ends up, pressing gently into cream cheese mixture to secure.

PIPE remaining cream cheese mixture onto bottom tips of berries.

Candy Cane Peppermint Kiss Cookies
from The Gardening Cook

Ingredients
1 1/2 cups powdered sugar
1 1/4 cup unsalted butter, at room temperature
1/2 tsp peppermint extract
1 tsp pure vanilla extract
1 large egg (I use free range eggs)
3 cups all-purpose flour
1 tsp baking powder
1/2 tsp Kosher salt
1/2 cup finely chopped Candy Cane flavored Hershey's Kisses
granulated sugar
additional, unwrapped Candy Cane Kisses- about 36

Instructions
Preheat your oven to 350° F. Before you start, be sure there is some space in your freezer that will fit the cookie sheet.

In large mixing bowl, combine the powdered sugar, butter, extracts, and egg. Beat at medium speed, being sure to scrape the bowl often until the mixture becomes creamy (about 2-3 minutes).

In another bowl, whisk together the flour, baking powder and salt. Gradually add this to your wet ingredients and mix until well blended (1 – 2 minutes). The mixture will be dry and crumbly. Stir in the chopped candy cane kisses.

Butter your hands and shape the dough into 1-inch balls; roll in granulated sugar. Place the balls 1-inch apart on a cookie sheet. Bake in the preheated oven for 10 — 12 minutes or until set.

Immediately after they come out of the oven, press a Candy Cane Kiss in the center of each cookie.

Place the cookie sheet (with the cookies) immediately into the freezer so that the Kisses will set and keep their shape.

Store in an airtight container in the fridge for about a week. They will also keep well in the freezer.

*Note: Be sure to put the cookies in the freezer immediately after adding the kisses to them. If you don't, the heat of the cookie will melt the kiss and you won't have the same delightful looking cookie with the little kiss point in the middle.

Candy Cane Cookies
from 123 Homeschool 4 Me

1 cup butter
1 egg
1 teaspoon vanilla
1 cup powdered sugar
1 ½ teaspoons almond extract
2 ½ cups flour
1 teaspoon salt
½ cup granulated sugar
½ teaspoon red food coloring
1 cup crushed peppermint

Heat oven to 375 degrees. Mix thoroughly butter, egg, vanilla, powdered sugar, and flavoring. Blend in salt and flour. Divide dough in half and mix coloring in half of the dough. Shape into candy canes. Bake 9 minutes each. Sprinkle with crushed peppermint. Yield about 4 dozen.

Peppermint Candy Cane Fudge
from Crafty Morning

Ingredients
2 ¾ cups semi-sweet chocolate chips
1 14oz can sweetened condensed milk
Pinch of Salt
2 tbsp Unsalted Butter
½ tsp Peppermint Extract
3 – 4 Finely Chopped Mini Candy Canes

Directions
Line an 8x8 pan for a thicker fudge, or a 9x9 pan for a slightly thinner fudge, with wax or parchment paper.

In a saucepan over medium heat melt together the chocolate chips, sweetened condensed milk, salt, and butter, stirring constantly. Once melted take off the heat and stir in peppermint extract.

Sprinkle candy canes over top, cover with plastic wrap, and refrigerate until firm. About 4 hours. Then cut into 1-inch pieces. Enjoy!

Candy Cane Swirl Cheesecake
from Feels Like Home

Ingredients
1 1/2 cups vanilla wafer crumbs about 45 cookies
1 tablespoon sugar
1/4 cup butter melted
3 8-ounce pkg cream cheese softened - get the full fat cream cheese, not a low-fat version. You'll notice the difference in your finished cheesecake
3/4 cup sugar
1 1/2 teaspoons vanilla extract
3 eggs
42-ounce Hershey's Candy Cane Kisses (that's a whole 8 oz bag give or take a couple of Kisses)
1 tablespoon milk
Sweetened whipped cream

Directions
Heat oven to 350.

Stir together cookie crumbs and sugar.

Blend in melted butter.

Press crust mixture into bottom and 1/2-inch up sides of a 9-inch springform pan.

Bake 8 minutes; cool.

Beat cream cheese, sugar, and vanilla in a large bowl until smooth.

Add eggs, one at a time, completely incorporating each before adding another.

Set aside 1/4 cup butter; pour remaining batter into crust.

Unwrap Kisses. Place 30 candies and milk in a microwave-safe bowl. Microwave at 50% power for one minute, stir. If necessary, microwave in 15 second increments at 50% power until candies are melted and mixture is well blended when stirred.

Gradually blend reserved cheesecake batter with melted candies. Drop mixture by tablespoonfuls on top of plain cheesecake batter in crust. Gently swirl with knife for a marbled effect.

Bake 45 to 50 minutes until center is almost set. Remove from oven to wire rack. Separate pan from edges using a scraper or knife but allow cheesecake to rest in pan until completely cool.

When cheesecake is cool, remove sides of pan. Cover and refrigerate until well chilled.

Garnish with whipped cream and remaining Kisses.

Refrigerate leftovers.

Candy Cane Fudge Recipe
from The Jenny Evolution

Ingredients:
3 cups white chocolate chips (2 bags)
1 can (14 oz) sweetened condensed milk
1 teaspoon vanilla extract
1/2 cup crushed candy canes

Directions for fudge:
Step 1: Line a 9×9 baking dish with parchment or foil and grease with butter.

Step 2: Using a large saucepan, combine the white chocolate chips and sweetened condensed milk.

Step 3: Stir until all of the white chocolate chips have completely melted.

Step 4: Then add the vanilla extract and stir in the crushed candy canes.

Step 5: Transfer fudge to the baking dish and allow it to cool to room temperature, approximately one hour. Sprinkle more crushed candy cane on top.

Step 6: Transfer to the refrigerator and allow to set-up for another 3-4 hours.

Step 7: The fudge is really easy to make! And look how delicious it came out. Just wrap up in pretty packages if you're bringing them to a party!

Appendix B: Social Media Image Size Guide

All dimensions given in pixels.

FACEBOOK
Cover Photo: 820 x 310 (mobile 640 x 320)

Profile Image: 180 x 180 (smartphone 128 x 128)

Fan Page Cover Video 820 x 312

Shared Link: 484 x 252

Shared Square: 1200 will display at 470

Event Image: 1920 x 1080

Ad: 470 x 246 (computer); 560 x 292 (mobile); 254 x 113 (vertical)

Online Display Promotions: 470 x 470 (computer); 626 x 840 (mobile); 254 x 133 (horizontal)

LINKEDIN
Profile Image: 400 x 400

Background Image: 1584 x 396

Shared Image: 529 x 320

Shared Image w/link: 520 x 272

YOUTUBE
Channel Profile: 100 x 100

Channel Cover Photo: 2560 x 1440

Video Uploads: 1280 x 720

INSTAGRAM
Profile Image: 110 x 110

Photo Thumbnail: 161 x 161

Photo Size: 1080 x 1080

Landscape: 1080 x 566

Portrait: 1080 x 1350

Online Display Promotions: 1080 (square will appear 640); 1080 x 566 (horizontal will appear 600 x 400)

TWITTER
Header Photo: 1500 x 500

Profile Photo: 400 x 400 (displays at 200 x 200)

Timeline Photo: 1024 x 512

Twitter Cards: 800 x 418 pixels or 800 x 800

PINTEREST
Profile Image: 280 x 280

Giraffe Pin: 600 x 1560

Pin Sizes: 600 x 750 (portrait); 600 (square); 600 x 900 (optimal); 600 x 1200 (infographic — only one part will appear, clicking will be complete)

TUMBLER

Profile Image: 128 x 128

Image Posts: 500 x750

GOOGLE+

Profile Image: 250 x 250

Cover Image: 1084 x 610

Shared Image: 530 wide

Shared Link Image: 530 wide

ELLO

Banner Image: 1800 x 1300

Profile Image: 340 x 340

SNAPCHAT

Geofilter Image: 1080 x 1920

Chinese Social Media

WECHAT

Profile Photo: 200 x 200

Article Preview Header: 900 x 500

Article Preview Thumbnail: 400 x 400 (displays at 200 x 200)

Article Inline Image: 400 wide x any height

WEIBO

Cover Image: 920 x 300

Profile Picture: 200 x 200 (displays at 100 x 100)

Banner: 550 x 260

Instream: 120 x 120

Contest Preview: 288 x 288

Contest Picture: 640 x 640

Contest Poster: 570 wide

Prize Picture: 200 x 200

Appendix C: LINKS

Link Checker
Link Checker

For Chrome: https://chrome.google.com/webstore/detail/check-my-links/ojkcdipcgfaekbeaelaapakgnjflfglf?hl=en-GB (I know this is out of alpha order, but a good link deserves top billing, don't you think? ;)

Article Marketing Sites

http://goarticles.com/

http://internationalpractice.com/business/

http://thephantomwriters.com/index.php

http://www.articledashboard.com/

http://www.articlegarden.com/

http://www.articlesbase.com/

http://www.articleson.com/

http://www.sitepronews.com/

http://www.selfgrowth.com

http://marniemarcus.com/unplugged/facebook-ad-management/

http://www.isnare.com

http://www.ladypens.com/

http://www.promotionworld.com

http://www.writeandpublishyourbook.com/magazine/

https://contributor.yahoo.com/signup.shtml

http://www.ezinearticles.com

Auto Responder Services

AWeber: www.aweber.com/

Constant Contact: https://www.constantcontact.com/

Robly: https://app.robly.com/invite?rc=f56a53fb2ad6910f3e83ebda

Your Mailing List Provider: www.yourmailinglistprovider.com/

Books and Movies

The Baby Boomer/Millennial Divide: Making it work at work by Beverly Mahone: https://tinyurl.com/BBMD-BM

Complete Library of Entrepreneurial Wisdom by Ginger Marks: http://www.CLEWbook.com

Customer Service Skills for Success by Robert W Lucas: http://a.co/d/739PPNL

#Next Level Manners: Business Etiquette for Millennials by Rachel Isgar Ph.D.: http://a.co/cew7qB4

Presentational Skills for the Next Generation by Ginger Marks: https://www.DocUmeantPublishing.com

Greeting Card Companies

123Greetings: http://www.123greetings.com

American Greetings: http://www.americangreetings.com/

Blue Mountain: www.bluemountain.com/

Cyberkisses: http://www.cyberkisses.com/

Day Springs: www.dayspring.com/ecards/

Evite: www.evite.com

Hallmark: https://www.hallmark.com/

Jacquie Lawson: www.jacquielawson.com/

Just Wink: https://www.justwink.com/

Operation Write Home: http://operationwritehome.org/

Punchbowl Greetings: http://www.punchbowl.com/invitations/preview/5400a4b424e4b36a3e000029/5400a56bbf947f655a000111

Send Out Cards: www.sendoutcards.com/

Podcast Directories

Corante-Podcasting: http://podcasting.corante.com/ —Weblog with news and events related to podcasting.

Hipcast: http://www.hipcaStcom/ —Audio and video podcasting service. Includes news and on-line tour.

iTunes: https://www.apple.com/itunes/ —The iTunes Store puts thousands of free podcasts at your fingertips.

Lextext.com: How to Podcast RIAA Music Under License—http://blog.lextext.com/blog/_archives/2005/1/4/225172.html —Discussion of legal ways to podcast music. [Podcast is 5.3 MB in size]

The Liberated Syndication Network: http://www.libsyn.com/ —Full featured service tailored specifically for media Self-publishing and podcasting. Price is based on usage, changing monthly if needed.

NPR: http://www.npr.org/rss/podcast/podcast_directory.php —Over 50 public radio stations and producers are working with NPR to bring you podcasting.

Podcasting News: http://www.podcastingnews.com/ —Information relating to podcasting, a podcast directory, and a user forum.

SkypeCasters: http://www.henshall.com/blog/archives/001056.html —Introducing instructions for SkypeCasting, the solution for podcasters to create audio recordings from interviews and conference calls using Skype.

Skype Forums: https://answers.microsoft.com/en-us/skype/ —Recording a Skype Conversation-Discussion thread covering software, techniques, and legal tidbits.

Wikipedia: Podcast –http://en.wikipedia.org/wiki/Podcast —Encyclopedia entry covering basics of the topic.

Promotional Product Supply Companies

4imprint: https://www.4imprint.com —for free samples

Build a Sign: http://www.buildasign.com/

CafePress: www.cafepress.com/

Crown Awards: https://www.crownawards.com/

iPrint: https://www.iprint.com/estore/

Judie Glenn Inc: www.judieglenninc.com —ask for Tracey Arehart

Northwest Territorial Mint: http://custom.nwtmint.com/

Overnight Prints: http://www.overnightprints.com/

PC/Nametag®: http://www.pcnametag.com/

Promotional Products: www.promotionalproducts.org/ —Get free quotes from multiple vendors

Staples: www.StaplesPromotionalProducts.com

VistaPrint: www.Vistaprint.com

World Class Medals: http://www.worldclassmedals.com/

Zazzle: http://www.zazzle.com/custom/buttons

Quote Sources

Bartleby: http://www.bartleby.com/

Brainy Quote: http://www.brainyquote.com/quotes/keywords/resources.html

Leadership Now: http://www.leadershipnow.com/quotes.html

Quote Garden: http://www.quotegarden.com/index.html

Quoteland: http://www.quoteland.com/

The Quotations Page: http://www.quotationspage.com/

Think Exit: http://thinkexist.com/quotes/american_proverb/

Woopidoo!: http://www.woopidoo.com/

Stock Photos

Tiny Eye: http://www.tineye.com —Reverse image search

Adobe Stock: https://stock.adobe.com/

Alamy: http://www.alamy.com

Beinecke: http://beinecke.library.yale.edu/digitallibrary

Maps Download MrSid: http://memory.loc.gov/ammem/help/download_sid.html

Big Stock Photo: http://www.bigstockphoto.com

Bing: http://www.bing.com

Can Stock Photo: http://www.canstockphoto.com

CreStock: http://www.crestock.com

DepositPhotos: http://depositphotos.com

Digital Scriptorium: http://bancroft.berkeley.edu/digitalscriptorium —public domain

Dreamstime: https://www.dreamstime.com

EJ Photo: https://ejphoto.com/ —Nature photography

Flickr: https://www.flickr.com/ — Advanced Search (only search on commercial content etc.)

Foto Search: http://www.fotosearch.com

Free Digital Photos: http://www.freedigitalphotos.net

Free Photo: http://www.freefoto.com/index.jsp

Getty: http://www.gettyimages.com/

Google: http://www.images.google.com — Use Advanced Search for Usage Rights, labeled with commercial w/modifications

Icon Finder: http://www.iconfinder.com/illustrations

iStockPhoto: http://www.iStockPhoto.com

Jupiter: http://www.jupiterimages.com

Library of Congress: http://www.loc.gov/index.html — American Memory and Prints and Photographs sections

Morguefile: http://morguefile.com

PhotoSpin: https://www.photospin.com/Default.asp?

Pixabay: http://pixabay.com/

Pixadus: http://pixdaus.com

RGB Stock: https://www.rgbstock.com/ — more than 95,000 high quality free stock photos, graphics for illustrations, wallpapers, and backgrounds

Scriptorium: http://www.scriptorium.columbia.edu/ public domain

Shutterstock: http://www.shutterstock.com

Stockxchg (FreeImages): http://www.sxc.hu/

ThinkStock Photos: http://www.thinkstockphotos.com/

Top Left Pixel: http://wvs.topleftpixel.com

VectorStock: https://www.vectorstock.com/royalty-free-vectors

Visipix: http://www.visipix.com — lots of Japanese art

Visual Photos: http://www.visualphotos.com

Watercolor Textures: https://lostandtaken.com/downloads/category/paint/watercolor-texture/

WebStockPro: http://www.webstockpro.com/

Wikimedia Commons: http://commons.wikimedia.org/wiki/Main_Page —Check images via languages

Wikipedia: https://en.wikipedia.org/wiki/Wikipedia:Public_domain_image_resources

You Work for Them: https://www.youworkforthem.com

Teleconference Companies

What is: www.business.com/directory/telecommunications/business_solutions/conferencing/

Buyer's Guide: www.buyerzone.com/telecom_services/telecon_services/buyers_guide5.html

Free Conference: www.freeconference.com/

Teleconference Live: http://teleconference.liveoffice.com

Teleconferencing Services: www.teleconferencingservices.net/

Yugma Desktop Sharing Software: http://vur.me/gmarks/Yugma/

Zoom: https://www.zoom.us

Virtual Assistant Companies

A Clayton's Secretary (Kathie M Thomas): http://vadirectory.net/

Streamline Your Marketing (Crystal Pina): https://streamlineyourmarketing.com/

Webinar Services

Adobe Acrobat Connect Pro: http://tryit.adobe.com/us/connectpro/universalvoice/?sdid=DNOSU

BrainShark: http://brainshark.com/

Cisco WebEx: http://webex.com/

ClickMeeting: https://clickmeeting.com/

Elluminate: http://www.elluminate.com/Products/?id=3

Facebook Live: https://live.fb.com/

Freebinar: http://www.freebinar.com/

Free Conference Calling: http://www.freeconferencecalling.com/

Fuze: http://www.fuzemeeting.com/

GatherPlace: http://www.gatherplace.net/start/

Google+ Hangouts: https://plus.google.com/hangouts

GoToMeeting: https://www.gotomeeting.com/

GoToWebinar: http://www.gotomeeting.com/fec/webinar

IBM Lotus Unyte: https://www.unyte.net/

iLinc: http://www.ilinc.com/

Infinite Conference: http://www.infiniteconference.com/

InstantPresenter: http://www.instantpresenter.com/

Intercall: http://www.intercall.com/smb/

Mega Meeting: http://www.megameeting.com/professional.html

Nefsis: http://www.nefsis.com/

ReadyTalk: https://www.readytalk.com/

Saba Centra: http://saba.com/

SalesForce: https://www.salesforce.com/

StageToWeb: http://www.omnovia.com/webcasting/

Tokbox: http://tokbox.com/

Video Seminar Live: http://www.videoseminarlive.com/

Wix: http://www.wix.com/

Yugma: https://www.yugma.com/

Zoho: http://www.zoho.com/meeting/

Appendix D: RESOURCES

The Baby Boomer/Millennial Divide: Making it work at work by Beverly Mahone: https://tinyurl.com/BBMD-BM

Presentational Skills for the Next Generation by Ginger Marks: https://www.DocUmeantPublishing.com

The Adaptability Primer by Daniel Goleman and colleagues: https://www.keystepmedia.com/shop/adaptability-primer/#.X8FNaGhKiUl

Life Hacker: https://www.lifehacker.com.au/

Military Spouse Owned Businesses: https://www.militaryspouse.com/military-life/the-giant-list-of-military-spouse-owned-businesses/

National Goat Yoga: https://goatyoga.com/

Red Panda Facts: https://www.youtube.com/watch?v=op4DN5oRahg

US Black Chambers: https://usblackchambers.org/

Food Drive Resources

Feeding America: A network of more than 200 food banks supporting approximately 61,000 local charitable agencies and 70,000 programs which provide food directly to individuals and families in need. www.feedingamerica.org

USDA The Food and Nutrition Information Center has a myriad of resources and ideas for how to address hunger issues in your community. https://www.nal.usda.gov/main/

Share Our Strength: Information on hunger as well as other tips for how to hold a successful food drive: www.strength.org/get_involved/food_drive/

Meals On Wheels Association of America: Meals on Wheels represents some 5,000 local, community-based Senior Nutrition Programs, which provide well over one million meals to seniors who need them each day. Some programs serve meals at congregate locations like senior centers, some programs deliver meals directly. www.mowaa.org

How-to Guides on Food Stamp (SNAP) outreach, How to Feed A Hungry Family, Community Gardens and more www.CreateTheGood.org/how-to

If you found this book interesting, helpful, motivational, fun, or any of the other numerous adjectives that have been used to describe this award-winning book, I would love to read your comments. Please let others know what a valuable asset you have found by leaving your review on your favorite book seller website.

If you would like to have a personal coaching session on how you can use this book to market your business send Ginger an email at ginger.marks@documeantdesigns.com and let her know. This valuable coaching service can be purchased for $295.00 per year and includes personal one-on-one coaching four times per year.

Thank you!

About the Author

Being a business owner for most of her adult life, operating a multi–million-dollar surgical clinic and a local barbecue take-out to list just a couple, have given Ginger Marks the insight needed to assist business owners from all walks of life.

Ginger is the owner of the Calomar, LLC which holds her DocUmeant family of companies. The various entities all work towards a common goal that just happens to be their tagline; "We Make YOU Look GOOD!" Her services include both publishing and digital design assistance. She is proud of the fact that she is able to give high quality, efficient service at a remarkably reasonable rate. It is for this reason she chose to list her publishing company in New York City while residing in Florida.

When Ginger decided to embark on a writing career it was of no surprise to her mother, who herself is a published author. Her love for the arts is what spurred her to hone her talents as a digital designer, offering services to business owners and authors alike.

DocUmeant.net offers editing and writing services; DocUmeantDesigns.com, as you would guess, focuses on designs ranging from websites to book covers and layouts to buttons and business stationery needs; while DocUmeantPublishing.com's focus was begun with the self-published author in mind. Now with ten years of experience in publishing she has built her success in the global community.

Ginger is a member of DesignFirms where she is a top-rated designer, SPANpro (Small Publishers Association of North America), IBPA (International Book Publishers Association), DBW (Digital Book World), and is on the board of FAPA as VP Communications (Florida Authors and Publishers Association).

Most recently, Ginger was awarded for her generous contribution to internet business while helping others achieve their goals in publishing and marketing. The Golden Mouse Award was presented to her by Women In e-Commerce on Oct 28, 2016. In 2012 she was awarded VIP membership to Covington's Who's Who and her publishing company, DocUmeant Publishing, was awarded the 2012 and 2016 New York Award in the Publishing Consultants and Services category by the U.S. Commerce Association (USCA). She recently won the 2015 and 2016 Clearwater, FL Design Firm Award and has won book cover design awards and is a multiple award winner for her *Weird and Wacky Holiday Marketing Guide* from FAPA.

In her spare time, she loves to do crafts of all sorts and sing. And yes, she is a little wacky at times too which keeps her fun and inspiring. Ginger lives in Florida where she works side-by-side with her husband, Philip, who is VP Editing for DocUmeant Publishing.

To contact Ginger whether for publish, design, or interviews you may reach her at ginger.marks@documeantdesigns.com or at 727-565-2130.

Additional Works

by Ginger Marks

Visit DocUmeantPublishing for more information or to purchase her books.

https://www.DocUmeantPublishing.com

ISBN-13: 978-1937801779

The companion Playbook for the Annual *Weird and Wacky Holiday Marketing Guide* l will assist you in planning and tracking your holiday marketing success using the tools, tips, and resources found in the *Weird and Wacky Holiday Marketing Guide*.

- Easily plan and track your marketing
- Organized by month
- Room to write notes
- Track your success
- No expiration date! Start using any time.

Print: $12.97 Available at https://www.DocUmeantPublishing.com

Print ISBN: 978-0-9788831-4-0

eBook ISBN: 978-0-9832122-7-0

Much has changed over the years in the public speaking arena. We have so many new and challenging tools at our disposal that we are no longer consigned to countless hours to travel from city to city to share our knowledge.

The internet has opened the doors to people from all places and races. At the click of a button, you can share your information in many forms of multi-media. With the availability of hosting online conferences and collaborations in both text-only and A/V environments, as are offered by Skype Conference™, Hot Conference™ and desktop sharing applications such as Yugma™, as well as teleconferences, the modes and means are so plentiful that more and more savvy business owners are venturing into the public speaking arena.

It is a well thought out, concise, instructional manual written in a manner that all can comprehend. Within the contents of this guide, you will learn the skills necessary to enable you to present your information in such a way that you will capture the attention and hearts of your eager audience.

Available in Print $14.95

Also available in eBook $9.95

Back to Basics is a collection of articles designed to assist the new business owner to jump start their business or the seasoned profession to put the punch back into their chosen career. It begins with a two-part series on the Nuts and Bolts of Business Building and continues from there to the ever-important Marketing Basics. As marketing is an issue for each and every business owner no matter their business or circumstances this section is presented in three parts. This eBook comes in Kindle and PDF versions and at $2.99 it is a real bargain.

$2.99 eBook Edition

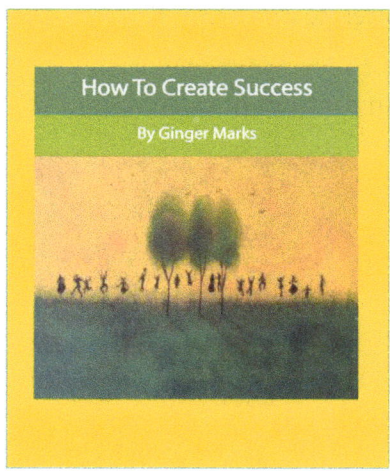

How To Create Success is the first eBook offering. Its bold colorful cover image entitled Jumping for Joy was designed by Amanda Tomasoa of Art by Amanda. The seven chapters contained within combine seven of the most highly rated articles written by Ginger at the time of publishing. One article Contagious Influence is currently the number one requested article and has been published in a magazine for writers titled 'Newbie News'. This is a free ebook and available for immediate download.

FREE: To download follow this link: http://www.gingermarksbooks.com/PDFs/HowToCreateSuccess.pdf.

SPECIAL REPORT

How to Create Long Sales Copy Web Pages

DocUmeant Designs.com

In this report you will learn how to create an effective Long Sales Copy Web Page and why you might need one. As you read through this report if you come to the conclusion that a Long Sales Copy Web Page is the right tool for your business, I highly recommend you use the company or individual with the working knowledge and integrity to create the site you need to get your important message across to your target market.

If you haven't a clue how to decipher who your target market is then that it the best place to start. Without this knowledge, no matter how compelling your product or service message is, it will result in an ineffective campaign. This will end up costing valuable time and money. Although this is beyond the context of this Special Report there are a myriad of resources available to you today online to help you along the way. As well, there are coaches who specialize in this area of expertise. Feel free to contact me and I will be happy to point you in the right direction.

To receive this FREE REPORT sign up for her monthly Words of Wisdom eZine at http://www.gingermarksbooks.com/.

Discover the 10 truths every business owner should know. Knowing and applying these truths will aide you in achieving your dream of entrepreneurship.

©2008 Ginger Marks All rights reserved.

To receive this eBook along with Ginger Marks' report *How to Create Long Sales Copy Web Pages* sign up for her monthly Words of Wisdom eZine here.

Get your copy of Ginger's Free Special Report: *10 Easy Steps to Re-purpose Your Content*.

This is the insider's view of how the *Complete Library of Entrepreneurial Wisdom* came about. With the information you will garner in this Special Report, you too can quickly and easily create your very own new money maker.

To download visit http://clewbook.com/

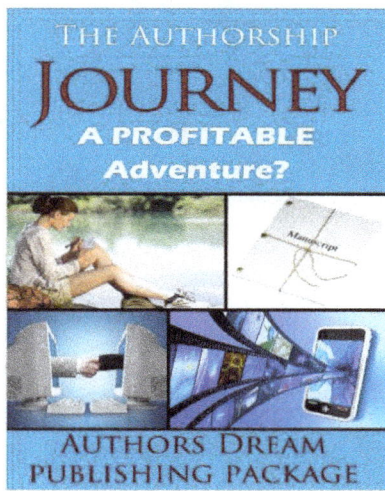

The Journey to Authorship is a road few travel. Find out how you too can traverse the challenges that lie ahead and come out on top. Advice from leading experts in the field.

Digital $0.99

Hardcover ISBN: 978-1937801380

Paperback ISBN: 978-1494928292

The Complete Library of Entrepreneurial Wisdom covers business basics, including how to and how not to start your business; marketing; marketing design, which is a topic rarely covered; writing, which covers technical, practical, as well as, marketing aspects to writing; and life reflections, such as planning for emergencies and disasters—both natural and man-made.

With over 150, power-packed, articles to choose from, the busy entrepreneur has at their fingertips, bite-sized training lessons to help them on their success journey. There is so much information packed into this book that it could well be the only book on core business issues that you will ever need.

$9.97 eBook

$32.95 Hardcover

$24.95 Paperback

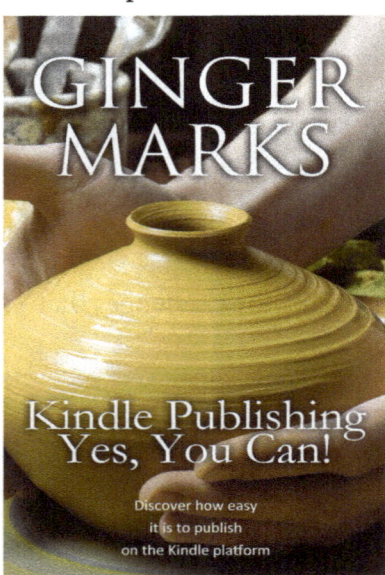

Publishing your ebook doesn't guarantee your book will look the way you intended it to. Even using the auto-generation tools can result in an ebook that isn't laid out the way you created it. In *Kindle*

Publishing, Yes You Can, Ginger Marks, publisher and designer, explains in easy terms exactly what you need to do and how to create an ebook that you will be proud to call your own.

Digital $2.99

Ginger's first children's picture book, *Mia's Reflections,* captures the heart of a young girl who learns that beauty is not just a pretty face, but rather a giving life.

Anticipating a new school with no friends, where she feels alone and ugly, young Mia prepares for her first day. She steps near her Grandmother's old Cheval mirror and there she senses her mama reaching out to her. "You're not ugly," her mama says. "You're beautiful." And she traces all the beautiful services Mia performs in a day. At last her mother appears in the mirror to give a fresh look at Mia's loveliness.

Followed by Parent/Teacher resources, this book will fill a young girl's day with thoughts of love and kindness.

$6.99 eBook Edition

$14.99 Print Edition (Feb 2019)

Book trailer: https://youtu.be/4DoQe9zp8LY

Weird and Wacky Holiday Marketing Guide Archive

Complete Your Collection Today!

Previous Editions Available here: http://www.HolidayMarketingGuide.com/past.html

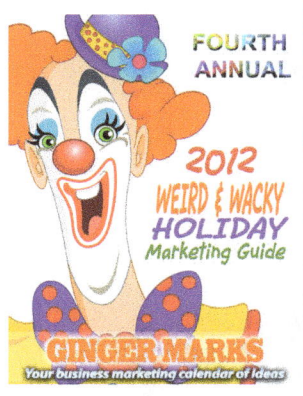
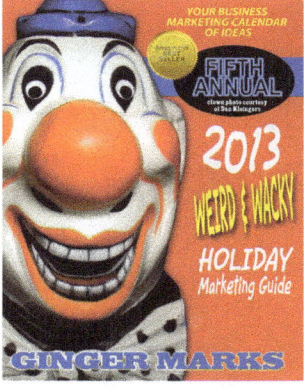

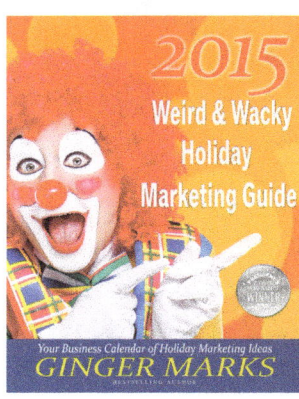
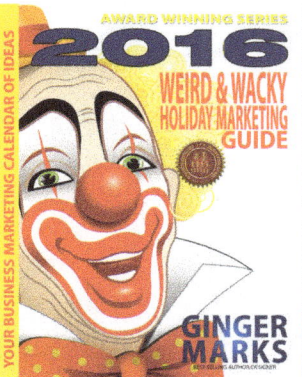
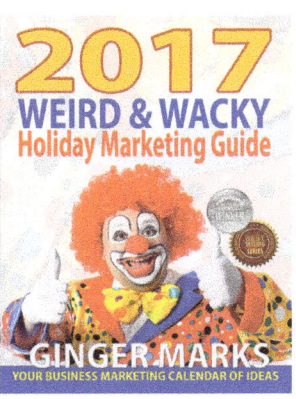

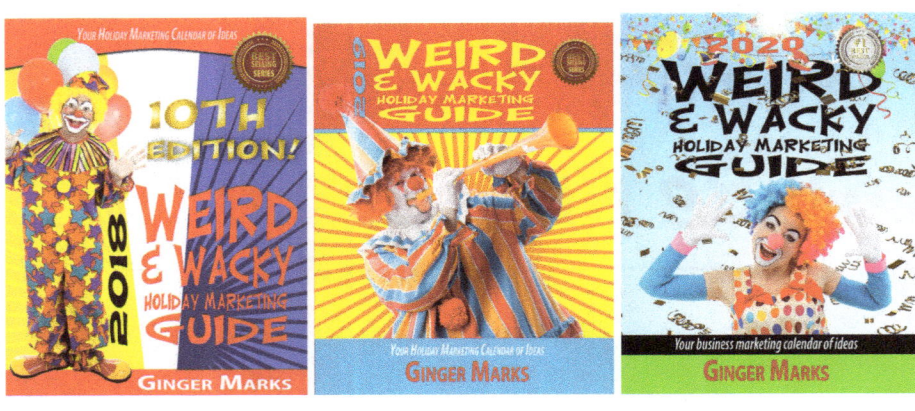
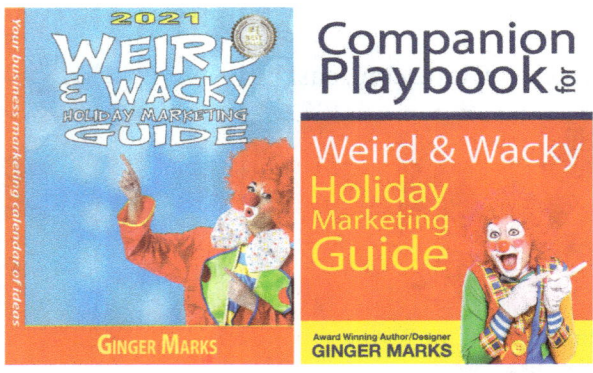

Affiliate Marketing Opportunities available at http://www.HolidayMarketingGuide.com!

Previous Editions Available at http://www.HolidayMarketingGuide.com/past.html

www.ingramcontent.com/pod-product-compliance
Lightning Source LLC
Chambersburg PA
CBHW081839170426
43199CB00017B/2786